W9-CPB-819

Algebra 1

HOLT, RINEHART AND WINSTON

A Harcourt Classroom Education Company

Austin · New York · Orlando · Atlanta · San Francisco · Boston · Dallas · Toronto · London

Photo Credit
Front Cover: (bckgd), Index Stock Photography Inc./Ron Russell; (b), Jean Miele MCMXCII/The Stock Market.

TestCheck is a trademark of Renaissance Learning.

Printed in the United States of America

ISBN 0-03-066373-3

5 6 7   082   05 04 03

Table of Contents

About the Algebra 1 Dynamic Test Generator with Electronic Testing and Grade Book ....**iv**

Getting Started Guide ....**vi**

Registering Your Copy of TestCheck™ ....**vii**

Lesson Objectives ....**ix**

Item Listing Printout

About the Algebra 1 Dynamic Test Generator with Electronic Testing and Grade Book

The Dynamic Test Generator with Electronic Testing and Grade Book CD-ROM can be found inside the back cover. The CD-ROM contains TestCheck™, which consists of three components—**Worksheet Builder** is a flexible test generator, **Management Module** performs all student/teacher/classroom gradebook functions, and **Student Module** allows students to take tests and review their performance on screen. Because TestCheck can be networked, teachers and administrators can share tests, worksheets, and student records on a local area network.

The **Worksheet Builder** can

- handle virtually all types of assessment items—multiple choice, free response, fill-in-the-blank, matching, true/false, and rubric-scored.
- generate different but equivalent items for each student using the patented algorithm and distractor-shuffling technology.
- create paper tests or on-screen tests, or output assessment items in an Internet-ready format.
- format assessments in many ways.
- allow teachers to add or edit questions through a powerful authoring tool.
- create Cartesian, polar, and line graphs using the function plotter tool.
- print worksheets, create separate answer sheets, and set due dates.

The **Management Module** makes grading and record keeping quick and easy, helping to track and record the history of each student and course. This module will quickly

- generate answer sheets.
- generate reports.
- establish class records.
- add students (manually or via an import function).
- set passwords.
- establish grading scales.
- view or print reports.

Reports may provide information on student history, student name, class history, class assignments, and class concept mastery.

The **Student Module** allows students to complete assignments, review them, and have them automatically scored—all on screen.

This supplement to *Algebra 1* contains

- the Algebra 1 Dynamic Test Generator with Electronic Testing and Grade Book.
- a Getting Started Guide, which includes installation instructions for the TestCheck system.
- objectives for each lesson in *Algebra 1*.
- a printed listing of all problem types that are contained in Worksheet Builder, the dynamic test generator.
- printed answers to prepared worksheets and chapter tests.

A mid-chapter test and three prepared chapter tests for each chapter can be found in electronic form on the CD-ROM.

TestCheck includes a user-friendly help system built into the program that assists you while you become familiar with the efficient use of each component. Most dialog boxes contain help buttons that access descriptive information, and you can also access the TestCheck help system from the main Help menu.

HRW has assembled a team of dedicated technical and teaching professionals and a comprehensive service program to provide you with the support you need. The following may be used to obtain technical support for any HRW software product.

Online Help: www.hrwtechsupport.com
email: tschrw@hrwtechsupport.com
HRW Technical Support Center: (800) 323-9239
7 A.M. to 10 P.M. Central Time on regular business days

Getting Started Guide

System Requirements
To run TestCheck on your computer it must meet the minimum system requirements listed below:

Microsoft Windows®
- 60 MHz Pentium processor-based computer
- 16 MB of installed RAM
- 50 MB of free disk space
- Microsoft Windows 95, 98, or NT
- CD-ROM drive

Macintosh®
- 66 MHz Power Macintosh
- 12 MB available RAM
- 50 MB of free disk space
- Mac OS 7.5.5 or later
- CD-ROM drive

Installing TestCheck™

Microsoft Windows®
1. Insert CD in CD-ROM drive. Once loaded, double-click on "My Computer" (on your desktop) and double-click on whichever drive shows the CD and "TestCheck."
2. Find the **Setup.exe** icon and double-click on it. This will begin the installation.
3. For the next three windows, simply accept the defaults and click [Next>] for each.
4. Once the setup is complete, * remove the disk, and restart your computer by clicking [Finish]. The TestCheck software is now loaded.

   *Note: The disk includes an online user's manual called *User's Guide* which requires Adobe Acrobat® Reader. If you do not already have this program on your computer, it is provided for you on the disk. Look for the **Ar40eng.exe** icon to install that as well.

Macintosh®
1. Insert CD in drive. When the TestCheck icon appears on the desktop, double-click to open.
2. Double-click on the TestCheck 2.0 Install icon.
3. Click [Continue] on the Welcome! screen.
4. Click [Install] to load all components.
5. Click [Install] again to load to the Hard Drive.
6. If Adobe Acrobat® Reader is not installed on your computer, click [OK] on this screen and then [Install] on the next to load it. (You'll need AR to open the online *User's Guide*.)
7. Once installation is complete, click [Quit], and finally, [Restart].

Network Installation

When installing TestCheck on a network system, be sure the data location selected is on the network server. This will allow every workstation with TestCheck installed to access the student database. Each individual workstation must have TestCheck individually installed but pointed toward the same data location on the network. For ease of use in the future it is strongly recommended that you now record the path to, and the name of, the data location.

TestCheck has a 400-student limit for each data location. To increase student capacity you will have to create additional data locations on the server, in completely different folders.

Registering Your Copy of TestCheck™

1. From the Start button, go to Programs, then TestCheck. Select TestCheck - Management. *Mac Users:* From either Launcher or the Hard Drive, open the TestCheck folder, and select TestCheck™ Management.

2. Follow system prompts until New Registration appears. Enter your school's name and location, and then your name in the appropriate fields. Click [Next>].

3. The next panel that appears is Data Location Choices (see below). If you wish to create a new folder for your data location, select the "Create a new location for data" option. TestCheck will automatically create a special database in this location that will allow you to share data with multiple computers. This panel also gives you the option of selecting an existing folder. This would only be applicable if your school maintained a compatible student database or owned a previous version of TestCheck. The sample data provided may be used to become familiar with the program itself.

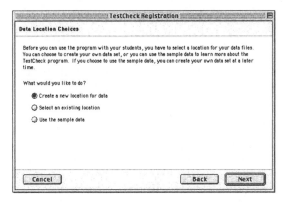

To select a data option, click the radio button in front of your choice, then click the [Next] button.

4. When the Select Location panel appears, click the [Select Location] button.

5. In the dialog box that follows, select the specific folder you wish to use for your TestCheck data. (To create a new folder on the Macintosh, click the [New folder] button.

In Windows, click the New Folder icon 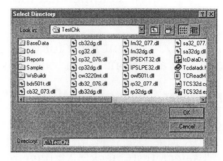. Name the folder, open it, then select it for the data location.)

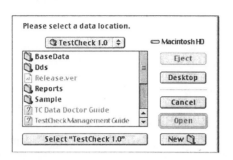

6. After selecting the appropriate location for your data, click [Select "Folder Name"] for Macintosh, or [OK] for Windows. This will return you to the Select Location panel of the Registration Assistant and display your information. Click [Next] to continue.

7. Click [Finish] or [Done] to complete the registration. The TestCheck Management module will automatically begin but requires a password.

8. The default administrator password is **admin**, but see Chapter 5 of the *User's Guide* for more information about setting user passwords. Click [OK].

9. You are now ready to begin using the software.

The Sample Data

Previewing TestCheck through use of the Sample Data is an excellent way to introduce yourself to the application. Perhaps you chose to do this in Step 3 during Data Location Choices, but now you want to select your *permanent* location. To return to the proper panel and initiate this procedure, follow these easy steps:

• Open TestCheck Management and click [School]

• Click [Preferences] and then double-click on [Data Location] to return to the Data Location Choices screen. Make your new selection and proceed as before.

Lesson Objectives

Chapter 1 - From Patterns To Algebra
Lesson 1 - Using Differences to Identify Patterns
    Objective 1 - Use differences to identify patterns in number sequences.
    Objective 2 - Make predictions by using patterns in number sequences.
Lesson 2 - Variables, Expressions, and Equations
    Objective 1 - Use variables to represent unknown quantities.
    Objective 2 - Represent real-world situations with equations and solve by
        guess-and-check.
Lesson 3 - The Algebraic Order of Operations
    Objective 1 - Apply the algebraic order of operations.
Lesson 4 - Graphing With Coordinates
    Objective 1 - Plot points and lines on a coordinate plane.
Lesson 5 - Representing Linear Patterns
    Objective 1 - Represent linear patterns with equations.
    Objective 2 - Represent linear equations with graphs.
Lesson 6 - Scatter Plots and Lines of Best Fit
    Objective 1 - Interpret data in a scatter plot.
    Objective 2 - Find a line of best fit on a scatter plot by inspection.

Chapter 2 - Operations In Algebra
Lesson 1 - The Real Numbers and Absolute Value
    Objective 1 - Compare real numbers.
    Objective 2 - Simplify expressions involving opposites and absolute value.
Lesson 2 - Adding Real Numbers
    Objective 1 - Use algebra tiles to model addition.
    Objective 2 - Add numbers with like signs.
    Objective 3 - Add numbers with unlike signs.
Lesson 3 - Subtracting Real Numbers
    Objective 1 - Use algebra tiles to model subtraction.
    Objective 2 - Define subtraction in terms of addition.
    Objective 3 - Subtract numbers with like and unlike signs.
Lesson 4 - Multiplying and Dividing Real Numbers
    Objective 1 - Multiply and divide positive and negative numbers.
    Objective 2 - Define the Properties of Zero.
Lesson 5 - Properties and Mental Computation
    Objective 1 - State and apply the Commutative, Associative, and Distributive
        Properties.
    Objective 2 - Use the Commutative, Associative, and Distributive Properties to
        perform mental computations.
Lesson 6 - Adding and Subtracting Expressions
    Objective 1 - Use the Distributive Property to combine like terms.
    Objective 2 - Simplify expressions with several variables.
Lesson 7 - Multiplying and Dividing Expressions
    Objective 1 - Multiply expressions containing variables.
    Objective 2 - Divide expressions containing variables.

Chapter 3 - Equations

Lesson 1 - Solving Equations by Adding and Subtracting
   Objective 1 - Solve equations by using addition and subtraction.
Lesson 2 - Solving Equations by Multiplying and Dividing
   Objective 1 - Solve equations by using multiplication and division.
Lesson 3 - Solving Two-Step Equations
   Objective 1 - Write equations that represent real-world situations.
   Objective 2 - Solve two-step equations.
Lesson 4 - Solving Multistep Equations
   Objective 1 - Write and solve multistep equations.
Lesson 5 - Using the Distributive Property
   Objective 1 - Use the Distributive Property to solve equations.
   Objective 2 - Solve real-world problems by using multistep equations.
Lesson 6 - Using Formulas and Literal Equations
   Objective 1 - Solve literal equations for a specific variable.
   Objective 2 - Use formulas to solve problems.

Chapter 4 - Proportional Reasoning and Statistics

Lesson 1 - Using Proportional Reasoning
   Objective 1 - Identify the means and extremes of a proportion.
   Objective 2 - Use proportions to solve problems.
Lesson 2 - Percent Problems
   Objective 1 - Find equivalent fractions, decimals, and percents.
   Objective 2 - Solve problems involving percent.
Lesson 3 - Introduction to Probability
   Objective 1 - Find the experimental probability that an event will occur.
Lesson 4 - Measures of Central Tendency
   Objective 1 - Find the mean, median, mode, and range of a data set.
   Objective 2 - Represent data with frequency tables.
Lesson 5 - Graphing Data
   Objective 1 - Interpret line graphs, bar graphs, and circle graphs.
   Objective 2 - Represent data with circle graphs.
   Objective 3 - Analyze graphs in order to find a misleading presentation of data.
Lesson 6 - Other Data Displays
   Objective 1 - Interpret stem-and-leaf plots, histograms, and box-and-
                 whisker plots.
   Objective 2 - Represent data with stem-and-leaf plots, histograms, and
                 box-and-whisker plots.

Chapter 14 - Functions and Transformations

Lesson 1 - Graphing Functions and Relations

Objective 1 - Use models to understand functions and relations.

Objective 2 - Evaluate functions by using function rules.

Objective 3 - Identify the parent functions of some important families of functions.

Lesson 2 - Translations

Objective 1 - Describe how changes to the rule of a function correspond to the translation of its graph.

Lesson 3 - Stretches and Compressions

Objective 1 - Describe how changes to the rule of a function stretch or compress its graph.

Lesson 4 - Reflections

Objective 1 - Describe how a change to the rule of a function corresponds to a reflection of its graph.

Lesson 5 - Combining Transformations

Objective 1 - Study a real-world application of transformed functions.

Objective 2 - Graph functions that involve more than one transformation.

Lesson 1: Using Differences to Identify Patterns

Objective 1: Use differences to identify patterns in number sequences.

[1.1.1.1] *Dynamic Item*

1. Which number is next in the sequence 117, 114, 111, 108, 105, ____ ?

   [A] 101　　　　　[B] 102　　　　　[C] 103　　　　　[D] 108

[1.1.1.2] *Dynamic Item*

2. If the second differences of a sequence are a constant of 3, the first of the first differences is 6, and the first term is 4, which are the first five terms of the sequence?

   [A] 4, 10, 19, 28, 37　　　　　　　[B] 4, 10, 19, 31, 46

   [C] 4, 10, 22, 40, 64　　　　　　　[D] 4, 10, 16, 22, 28

[1.1.1.3] *Dynamic Item*

3. What are the first four terms of the sequence with a constant difference of 12 and a first term of 33?

[1.1.1.4] *Dynamic Item*

4. A piece of machinery valued at $80,000 depreciates $6000 the first year, $5700 the second year, $5400 the third year, and so on. Complete the table to find all of the first differences, the set of second differences and the value of the machinery at the end of the fifth year.

Value	$80,000	$74,000	$68,300	$62,900	
First Differences	−$6000	−$5700	−$5400		
Second Differences					

Lesson 1: Using Differences to Identify Patterns

Objective 2: Make predictions by using patterns in number sequences.

[1.1.2.5] *Dynamic Item*

5. The following table shows the total cost of belonging to Fitness Fantasy Health Club for 4 months. If the table continues in the same pattern, what is the total cost during the 7th month?

Month	1	2	3	4
Total Cost	$190	$230	$270	$310

   [A] $280   [B] $580   [C] $1330   [D] $430

[1.1.2.6] *Dynamic Item*

6. This table indicates how rapidly water evaporates from an open 620-gallon tank.

Days	Remaining Water (gallons)
0	620
10	600
20	580
30	560

   How much water is left at the end of 90 days?

   [A] 440 gallons   [B] 540 gallons   [C] 430 gallons   [D] 420 gallons

[1.1.2.7] *Dynamic Item*

7. The distance in feet that a free-falling body falls in each second, starting with the first second, is given by the sequence 19, 57, 95, 133, ... Find the distance that the body falls in the 6th second.

Lesson 1: Using Differences to Identify Patterns

[1.1.2.8] *Dynamic Item*

8. The following chart shows the charges Paloma's Plumbing makes for a home repair call based on the number of hours worked. If the pattern continues, how much would she charge for a full 8-hour day's work?

Hours Worked	1	2	3	4
Amount Charged	$85	$120	$155	$190

Lesson 2: Variables, Expressions, and Equations

Objective 1: Use variables to represent unknown quantities.

[1.2.1.9] *Dynamic Item*

9. The cost of a school banquet is $80 + $15n, where n is the number of people attending. Which is the cost for 60 people?

[A] $155   [B] $979   [C] $980   [D] $154

[1.2.1.10] *Dynamic Item*

10. If $b = 5$, which is the value of $8b - 3$?   [A] 37   [B] 65   [C] 16   [D] –19

[1.2.1.11] *Dynamic Item*

11. Complete the table of values for $y = 9x + 3$.

x	1	2	3	4	5
y					

[1.2.1.12] *Dynamic Item*

12. Write an algebraic expression that represents "three orange crates, each containing x oranges, decreased by 17 oranges."

Lesson 2: Variables, Expressions, and Equations

Objective 2: Represent real-world situations with equations and solve by guess-and-check.

[1.2.2.13] *Dynamic Item*

13. Erik pays $268 in advance on his account at the athletic club. Each time he uses the club, $9 is deducted from the account. Which equation represents the value remaining in his account after x visits to the club, and which is the amount remaining in the account after 9 visits?

    [A] $V = 268 - 9x;$ $187

    [B] $V = 9 - 268x;$ $187

    [C] $V = 268 - 9x;$ $178

    [D] $V = (268 - 9)x;$ $192

[1.2.2.14] *Dynamic Item*

14. Which problem could be solved using the equation $136 - t = 22$?

    [A] Find a number t decreased by 22 that equals 136.

    [B] There were 136 toys donated to the program. 22 more toys were donated. Find t, the total number of toys.

    [C] There were 136 tickets to sell before opening night. t tickets were sold. There were 22 left. How many tickets were sold?

    [D] 22 is less than 136 and t.

[1.2.2.15] *Dynamic Item*

15. An employee receives a weekly salary of $350 and a 5% commission on all sales. Write an equation to find her total weekly earnings if p represents the total amount earned weekly and s represents the total weekly sales. Find her earnings for a week with $2677 total sales.

[1.2.2.16] *Dynamic Item*

16. Imagine that you own your own tee-shirt business. The cost of making the designs and buying the tee shirts is $475. In addition to these one time charges, the cost of printing each shirt is $2.50. Write an equation showing the total cost, C, to manufacture x tee shirts and find the total cost to manufacture 100 shirts.

Lesson 3: The Algebraic Order of Operations

Objective 1: Apply the algebraic order of operations.

[1.3.1.17] *Dynamic Item*

17. Evaluate $5\left(5n+2p\right)^2$ for $n=1$ and $p=1$.

    [A] 145   [B] 245   [C] 45   [D] 580

[1.3.1.18] *Dynamic Item*

18. Evaluate the expression.   [A] 25   [B] 149   [C] 125   [D] 145

    $\left[31-\left(4+2\right)\right]\cdot 5$

[1.3.1.19] *Dynamic Item*

19. Evaluate the expression.

    $27 \div 3^2 - 3 + 2^4$ 16

[1.3.1.20] *Dynamic Item*

20. Evaluate the expression.

    $\dfrac{75 \cdot 5^2 - 3 \cdot 2^2}{2 + 5^2}$ 69

Lesson 4: Graphing With Coordinates

Objective 1: Plot points and lines on a coordinate plane.

[1.4.1.21] *Dynamic Item*

21. The table below shows the water depth of a pond in summer over time.

Water Level	
Time (week)	Depth
1	8.63
2	6.63
3	4.75
4	2.25
5	0.13

Graph the ordered pairs and make a statement about the trend that can be seen.

[A]

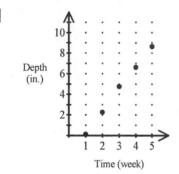

The depth of the water decreases over time.

[B]

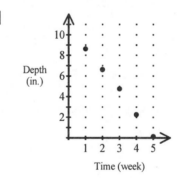

The depth of the water increases over time.

[C]

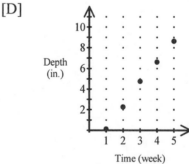

The depth of the water decreases over time.

[D]

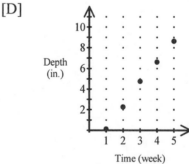

The depth of the water increases over time.

Lesson 4: Graphing With Coordinates

[1.4.1.22] *Dynamic Item*

22. Complete the table and select the graph which shows the ordered pairs from the table and the line that represents the equation.

$y = x - 2$

x	y
0	
1	
2	
3	
4	

[A]
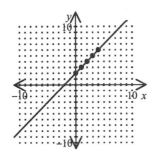

[B]
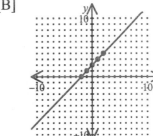

[C]
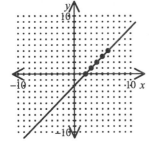

[D]
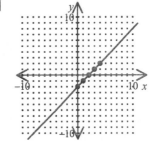

Lesson 4: Graphing With Coordinates

[1.4.1.23] *Dynamic Item*

23. What are the coordinates of point A? In which quadrant is point A located?

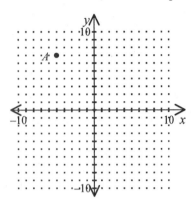

[1.4.1.24] *Dynamic Item*

24. Complete the table and graph the line for $y = 2x - 1$.

x	1	2	3	4	5
y					

Lesson 5: Representing Linear Patterns

Objective 1: Represent linear patterns with equations.

[1.5.1.25] *Dynamic Item*

25. A paper airplane is sailed off a 89-foot-high bridge. As the paper airplane flies, its height decreases at a steady rate.

Time (sec)	0	1	2	3	4	5
Height (ft)	89	81	73	65	57	49

Which equation describes the relationship between time (t) and height (h)?

[A] $h = 8t - 89$ [B] $h = 1.6t - 89$ [C] $h = 89 - 8t$ [D] $h = 89 - 1.6t$

Lesson 5: Representing Linear Patterns

[1.5.1.26] *Dynamic Item*

26. Use the table to find the first difference and the equation that represents the data in the table.

x	0	1	2	3	4	5
y	2	5	8	11	14	17

[A] First difference is –3.
$y = -3x - 2$

[B] First difference is 3.
$y = -3x + 2$

[C] First difference is –3.
$y = 3x - 2$

[D] First difference is 3.
$y = 3x + 2$

[1.5.1.27] *Dynamic Item*

27. Find the first differences for the table of values and write an equation representing the pattern.

x	0	1	2	3	4	5	6	7
y	5	9	13	17	21	25	29	33

[1.5.1.28] *Dynamic Item*

28. a. The mass of a box is 250 grams. Inside the box are cubes that each have a mass of 20 grams. Make a table of values for the total mass of the box if it contains 1 cube, 2 cubes, 3 cubes, 4 cubes, and 5 cubes.
b. Write an equation for the relationship between the number of cubes, n, and the total mass of the box and the cubes, T.
c. Use the equation in part b. to find the mass of the box when it contains 50 cubes.

Lesson 5: Representing Linear Patterns

Objective 2: Represent linear equations with graphs.

[1.5.2.29] *Dynamic Item*

29. Using the graph, complete the table of values then determine which of the following is the equation of the line graphed?

x	1	2	3	4	5
y					

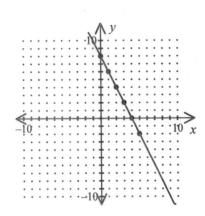

[A] $y = 7 - 2x$ [B] $y = 8 - 4x$ [C] $y = 9 - 2x$ [D] $y = 8 - 2x$

Lesson 5: Representing Linear Patterns

[1.5.2.30] *Dynamic Item*

30. Complete the table of values for $y = 4x + 6$, then identify which of the following is the graph of the equation.

x	1	2	3	4
y				

[A]
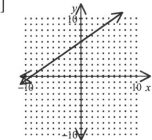

[B]
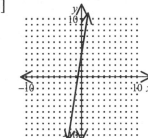

[C]
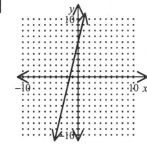

[D]
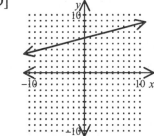

[1.5.2.31] *Dynamic Item*

31. Model the following situation with an equation and a graph: A music club membership costs $8.00 and $6.00 per CD.

[1.5.2.32] *Dynamic Item*

32. Make a table of values for $y = x + 1$ using 1, 2, 3, 4 and 5 as values for x. Draw a graph for the equation by plotting points from your data set.

x	1	2	3	4	5
y					

Lesson 6: Scatter Plots and Lines of Best Fit

Objective 1: Interpret data in a scatter plot.

[1.6.1.33] *Dynamic Item*

33. Which of the scatter plots shows little or no relationship?

[A]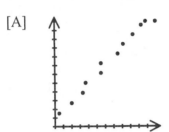

[B]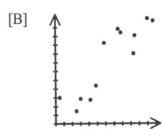

[C]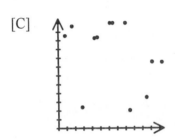

[D]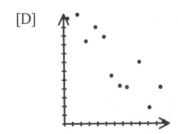

[1.6.1.34] *Dynamic Item*

34. A radio disc jockey kept track of the number of requests for songs by a certain artist, and the time of day the request calls were made. The data is displayed below:

Number of Requests	9	0	0	10	5	10	1	5
Time of Day	2 p.m.	3 p.m.	4 p.m.	5 p.m.	6 p.m.	7 p.m.	8 p.m.	9 p.m.

If the data were displayed on a scatter plot, which of the following describes the correlation between the two variables?

[A] There is a positive correlation.

[B] There is no correlation.

[C] There is a negative correlation.

[D] There is a weak negative correlation.

Lesson 6: Scatter Plots and Lines of Best Fit

[1.6.1.35] *Dynamic Item*

35. The table below shows the height of a bamboo plant over time.

Bamboo Height	
Week	Height (in.)
1	2.00
2	4.38
3	6.63
4	9.00
5	10.25

   Make a scatter plot to show the relationship between time and height. Describe the relationship.

[1.6.1.36] *Dynamic Item*

36. Make a scatter plot that shows the correlation for the length of someone's hair compared to his income.

Lesson 6: Scatter Plots and Lines of Best Fit

Objective 2: Find a line of best fit on a scatter plot by inspection.

[1.6.2.37] *Dynamic Item*

37. The table shows Christine's best javelin throws each year. Display the data on a scatter plot of distance versus year. Draw a line of best fit.

Year	1989	1990	1991	1992	1993	1994	1995	1996
Distance (m)	41.5	43.125	44	47	47.5	48.375	51.375	51.625

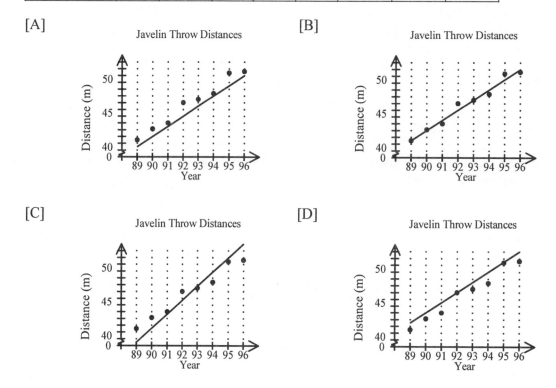

Lesson 6: Scatter Plots and Lines of Best Fit

[1.6.2.38] *Dynamic Item*

38. The graph shows the price of a gallon of unleaded gasoline at randomly selected stations.

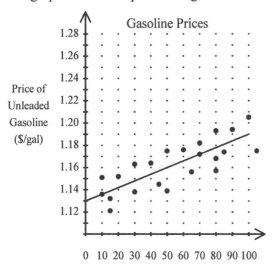

Use the line of best fit to give the price of a gallon of gasoline 10 miles from town.

[A] $1.16   [B] $1.10   [C] $1.14   [D] $1.12

[1.6.2.39] *Dynamic Item*

39. The table shows the time spent researching the stock market each week and the percent gain for an investor.

Research Time (hours)	6	8	10	12	14	16	18
Gain (%)	20	32	32	35	44	59	50

Draw a scatter plot of gain versus research time. Draw a line of best fit. Then, estimate the percent gain from researching the stock market for 20 hours.

Lesson 6: Scatter Plots and Lines of Best Fit

[1.6.2.40] *Dynamic Item*

40. The table shows the relationship between the time a student spends typing each week and his percent improvement on speed assessments.

Practice Hours	6	8	10	12	14	16	18
Percent Improvement	17	24	37	35	45	49	62

Make a scatter plot of percent improvement vs. practice hours and then draw the line of best fit. Using the line of best fit, estimate what percent gain would be expected if the number of practice hours is 11 hours.

Lesson 1:   Using Differences to Identify Patterns

Objective 1: Use differences to identify patterns in number sequences.

[1.1.1.1] *Dynamic Item*

[1]   [B]

[1.1.1.2] *Dynamic Item*

[2]   [B]

[1.1.1.3] *Dynamic Item*

[3]   33, 45, 57, 69

[1.1.1.4] *Dynamic Item*

[4]

Value	$80,000	$74,000	$68,300	$62,900	$57,800
First Differences	$-$6000	$-$5700	$-$5400	$-$5100	$-$4800
Second Differences	$-$300	$-$300	$-$300	$-$300	$-$300

Objective 2: Make predictions by using patterns in number sequences.

[1.1.2.5] *Dynamic Item*

[5]   [D]

[1.1.2.6] *Dynamic Item*

[6]   [A]

[1.1.2.7] *Dynamic Item*

[7]   209 ft

[1.1.2.8] *Dynamic Item*

[8] $330

Lesson 2: Variables, Expressions, and Equations

Objective 1: Use variables to represent unknown quantities.

[1.2.1.9] *Dynamic Item*

[9] [C]

[1.2.1.10] *Dynamic Item*

[10] [A]

[1.2.1.11] *Dynamic Item*

[11]

x	1	2	3	4	5
y	12	21	30	39	48

[1.2.1.12] *Dynamic Item*

[12] $3x - 17$

Objective 2: Represent real-world situations with equations and solve by guess-and-check.

[1.2.2.13] *Dynamic Item*

[13] [A]

[1.2.2.14] *Dynamic Item*

[14] [C]

[1.2.2.15] *Dynamic Item*

[15] $p = 0.05s + 350$; $483.85

[1.2.2.16] *Dynamic Item*

[16] $C = 2.50x + 475$; $725.00

Lesson 3:   The Algebraic Order of Operations

Objective 1: Apply the algebraic order of operations.

[1.3.1.17] *Dynamic Item*

[17] [B]

[1.3.1.18] *Dynamic Item*

[18] [C]

[1.3.1.19] *Dynamic Item*

[19] 16

[1.3.1.20] *Dynamic Item*

[20] 69

Lesson 4: Graphing With Coordinates

Objective 1: Plot points and lines on a coordinate plane.

[1.4.1.21] *Dynamic Item*

[21] [C]

[1.4.1.22] *Dynamic Item*

[22] [D]

[1.4.1.23] *Dynamic Item*

[23] (–5, 7); Quadrant II

[1.4.1.24] *Dynamic Item*

x	1	2	3	4	5
y	1	3	5	7	9

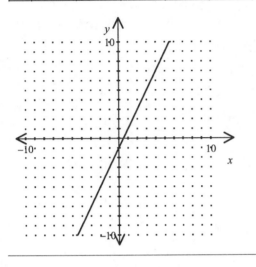

[24] _____

Lesson 5: Representing Linear Patterns

Objective 1: Represent linear patterns with equations.

[1.5.1.25] *Dynamic Item*

[25] [C]

[1.5.1.26] *Dynamic Item*

[26] [D]

[1.5.1.27] *Dynamic Item*

The first difference is 4.
$y = 4x + 5$

[27] _____

[1.5.1.28] *Dynamic Item*

a.

Number of Cubes	Total Mass of Cubes and Box (g)
1	270
2	290
3	310
4	330
5	350

b. $T = 250 + 20n$

[28]   c. 1250 g

Objective 2: Represent linear equations with graphs.

[1.5.2.29] *Dynamic Item*

[29]   [D]

[1.5.2.30] *Dynamic Item*

[30]   [C]

[1.5.2.31] *Dynamic Item*

$y = 6x + 8$

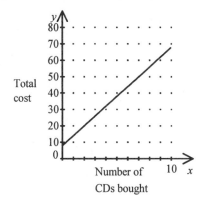

[31]

[1.5.2.32] *Dynamic Item*

x	1	2	3	4	5
y	2	3	4	5	6

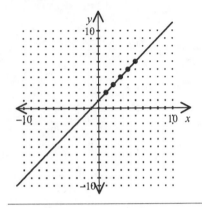

[32] _____

Lesson 6: Scatter Plots and Lines of Best Fit

Objective 1: Interpret data in a scatter plot.

[1.6.1.33] *Dynamic Item*

[33] [C]

[1.6.1.34] *Dynamic Item*

[34] [B]

[1.6.1.35] *Dynamic Item*

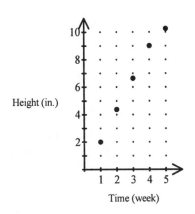

[35]   There is a positive correlation between time and the height of the plant.

[1.6.1.36] *Dynamic Item*

Sample answer: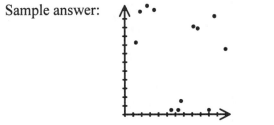

[36]   _____

Objective 2: Find a line of best fit on a scatter plot by inspection.

[1.6.2.37] *Dynamic Item*

[37]   [B]

[1.6.2.38] *Dynamic Item*

[38]   [C]

[1.6.2.39] *Dynamic Item*

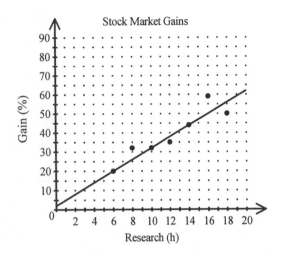

Stock Market Gains

[39]   62%

[1.6.2.40] *Dynamic Item*

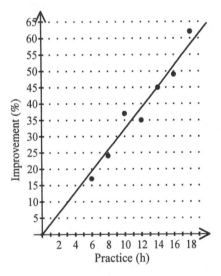

[40]   36%; Answers will vary

Lesson 1: The Real Numbers and Absolute Value

Objective 1: Compare real numbers.

[2.1.1.1] *Dynamic Item*

1. Which symbol, <, >, or =, would make the statement true? $-9\ \bigcirc\ -7$

    [A] <   [B] >   [C] =   [D] none of these

[2.1.1.2] *Dynamic Item*

2. Which symbol, <, >, or =, would make the statement true? $-\dfrac{1}{4}\ \bigcirc\ -\dfrac{3}{4}$

    [A] <   [B] >   [C] =   [D] none of these

[2.1.1.3] *Dynamic Item*

3. Write the numbers $-2.47,\ -\dfrac{6}{5},\ 20,\ \dfrac{5}{8}$ in order from least to greatest.

[2.1.1.4] *Dynamic Item*

4. Write an example of a rational number that is less than $-\dfrac{5}{6}$.

Objective 2: Simplify expressions involving opposites and absolute value.

[2.1.2.5] *Dynamic Item*

5. Which is the opposite of 17?   [A] −17   [B] $\dfrac{1}{17}$ [C] $-\dfrac{1}{17}$ [D] 17

[2.1.2.6] *Dynamic Item*

6. Simplify the expression.   [A] −10   [B] $-\dfrac{1}{10}$ [C] ±10   [D] 10
    $-|10|$

Algebra 1

Lesson 1: The Real Numbers and Absolute Value

[2.1.2.7] *Dynamic Item*

7. Simplify the expression.
$$\left|-10\right|+\left|-15\right|$$

[2.1.2.8] *Dynamic Item*

8. Simplify the expression.
$$-(-12)-|-8|+(-6)$$

Lesson 2: Adding Real Numbers

Objective 1: Use algebra tiles to model addition.

[2.2.1.9] *Dynamic Item*

9. Let one white tile equal +1 and one black tile equal –1. Which is the numerical expression for the model? Find the sum.

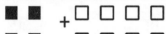

[A] –4 + 8; 4   [B] –4 + 8; –12   [C] 4 + 8; 12   [D] 4 + 8; –4

[2.2.1.10 *Dynamic Item*

10. Let one white tile equal +1 and one black tile equal –1. Which is the numerical expression for the model? Find the sum.

[A] 4 + (–5); –1   [B] –4 + 5; 1   [C] 4 + 5; 9   [D] –4 + (–5); –9

[2.2.1.11] *Dynamic Item*

11. Let one white tile equal +1 and one black tile equal –1. Represent the sum –6 + (–4) using algebra tiles.

Lesson 2: Adding Real Numbers

[2.2.1.12] *Dynamic Item*

12. Let one white tile equal +1 and one black tile equal –1. Use algebra tiles to represent the number 4 in two different ways. Draw a diagram.

Objective 2: Add numbers with like signs.

[2.2.2.13] *Dynamic Item*

13. Find the sum. [A] 32 [B] –98 [C] –32 [D] 98

$(-33)+(-65)$

[2.2.2.14] *Dynamic Item*

14. Find the sum. [A] $\dfrac{7}{18}$ [B] $\dfrac{23}{18}$ [C] $-\dfrac{23}{18}$ [D] $-\dfrac{7}{18}$

$-\dfrac{4}{9}+\left(-\dfrac{5}{6}\right)$

[2.2.2.15] *Dynamic Item*

15. Find the sum.
$-4.82+(-5.13)$

[2.2.2.16] *Dynamic Item*

16. Evaluate $x+y$ for $x=-3.6$ and $y=-13$.

Objective 3: Add numbers with unlike signs.

[2.2.3.17] *Dynamic Item*

17. Find the sum. [A] 3 [B] –85 [C] –3 [D] 85

$(-41)+(44)$

Lesson 2: Adding Real Numbers

[2.2.3.18] *Dynamic Item*

18. Evaluate $a + (-b)$ for $a = 39$ and $b = -47$.   [A] –86   [B] 86   [C] 8   [D] –8

[2.2.3.19] *Dynamic Item*

19. Find the sum.

$$\frac{2}{7} + -2\frac{3}{4}$$

[2.2.3.20] *Dynamic Item*

20. Evaluate $r + s + t + u$ for $r = 7.3$, $s = -2.1$, $t = 8.6$ and $u = 7.7$.

Lesson 3: Subtracting Real Numbers

Objective 1: Use algebra tiles to model subtraction.

[2.3.1.21] *Dynamic Item*

21. If one white tile represents +1 and one black tile represents –1, which subtraction equation does the following algebra-tile equation represent?

[A] $6 - (-7) = -1$ [B] $-7 - (-6) = -1$ [C] $-7 - 6 = -1$ [D] $-6 - (-7) = 1$

Lesson 3: Subtracting Real Numbers

[2.3.1.22] *Dynamic Item*

22. If one white tile represents +1 and one black tile represents −1, which subtraction equation does the following algebra-tile equation represent?

   [A] $-4-(-1)=-5$ [B] $1-(-4)=5$ [C] $-4-1=-5$ [D] $-1-4=-5$

[2.3.1.23] *Dynamic Item*

23. If one white tile represents +1 and one black tile represents −1, draw an algebra-tile equation to illustrate the equation. $-1-6=-7$

[2.3.1.24] *Dynamic Item*

24. If one white tile represents +1 and one black tile represents −1, draw an algebra-tile equation to illustrate the equation. $-4-(-7)=3$

Objective 2: Define subtraction in terms of addition.

[2.3.2.25] *Dynamic Item*

25. Rewrite the difference as a sum.
$3-(-9)$

   [A] $-3+(-9)$ [B] $-3+9$ [C] $3+(-9)$ [D] $3+9$

[2.3.2.26] *Dynamic Item*

26. Rewrite the difference as a sum.
$3-p$

   [A] $-3+(-p)$ [B] $3+p$ [C] $-3+p$ [D] $3+(-p)$

Lesson 3: Subtracting Real Numbers

[2.3.2.27] *Dynamic Item*

27. Rewrite the difference as a sum.

$7 - 6$

[2.3.2.28] *Dynamic Item*

28. Rewrite the difference as a sum.

$12 - (-13) + 10$

Objective 3: Subtract numbers with like and unlike signs.

[2.3.3.29] *Dynamic Item*

29. Find the difference.   [A] 31.963   [B] −16.25   [C] −11.867   [D] −11.99

$-16.737 - (-4.87)$

[2.3.3.30] *Dynamic Item*

30. Find the difference.   [A] $\dfrac{2}{5}$ [B] $\dfrac{6}{5}$ [C] $-\dfrac{6}{5}$ [D] $-\dfrac{2}{5}$

$\dfrac{4}{5} - \left(-\dfrac{2}{5}\right)$

[2.3.3.31] *Dynamic Item*

31. Evaluate $-v - w$ for $v = 40$ and $w = -23$.

[2.3.3.32] *Dynamic Item*

32. Find the distance between the points –7.1 and 5.6 on a number line.

Lesson 4: Multiplying and Dividing Real Numbers

Objective 1: Multiply and divide positive and negative numbers.

[2.4.1.33] *Dynamic Item*

33. Evaluate.   [A] $-\dfrac{158}{7}$ [B] $\dfrac{158}{7}$ [C] -24 [D] 24
    $28 \cdot (-6) \div 7$

[2.4.1.34] *Dynamic Item*

34. Evaluate.   [A] -16 [B] 0   [C] 16   [D] -8
    $(-4)(-4)$

[2.4.1.35] *Dynamic Item*

35. Find the quotient.
    $\dfrac{-4}{7} \div \dfrac{-28}{-4}$

[2.4.1.36] *Dynamic Item*

36. What is the reciprocal of $\dfrac{2}{7}$?

Objective 2: Define the Properties of Zero.

[2.4.2.37] *Dynamic Item*

37. Which of the following statements is true?

    [A] Zero divided by 2 is undefined.   [B] Negative 1 divided by 0 is 0.

    [C] Zero divided by 1 is 0.   [D] Zero multiplied by 1 is 1.

[2.4.2.38] *Dynamic Item*

38. Find the product or quotient.   [A] 14,805   [B] 1002   [C] 0   [D] 1
    $987 \cdot 15 \cdot 0$

Lesson 4: Multiplying and Dividing Real Numbers

[2.4.2.39] *Dynamic Item*

39. Find the product or quotient.

    $$\frac{6}{0}$$

[2.4.2.40] *Dynamic Item*

40. Is the following statement true or false? Explain.
    Zero divided by 1 is 0.

Lesson 5: Properties and Mental Computation

Objective 1: State and apply the Commutative, Associative, and Distributive Properties.

[2.5.1.41] *Dynamic Item*

41. Which property is illustrated by the following statement?
    $(8 \cdot 3) \cdot 9 = (3 \cdot 8) \cdot 9$

    [A] Commutative of Addition   [B] Commutative of Multiplication

    [C] Associative of Addition   [D] Associative of Multiplication

[2.5.1.42] *Dynamic Item*

42. Which of the following is an example of the Associative Property of Addition?

    [A] $1 + 3 = 3 + 1$ [B] $7 + (1 + 4) = 7 + (1 + 4)$

    [C] $1 + 2 = 3 + 0$ [D] $(6 + 12) + 2 = 6 + (12 + 2)$

[2.5.1.43] *Dynamic Item*

43. Use the Associative and Commutative Properties to find $(17 + 74) + 43$. Show your work and name the properties used.

Lesson 5: Properties and Mental Computation

[2.5.1.44] *Dynamic Item*

44. Use the Distributive Property to rewrite the expression $49bc - 7bd$.

Objective 2: Use the Commutative, Associative, and Distributive Properties to perform mental computation.

[2.5.2.45] *Dynamic Item*

45. Which two properties would correctly replace the two question marks to name the properties used in finding the sum of $27 + (45 + 173)$?

$27 + (173 + 45)$	?
$(27 + 173) + 45$	?
$200 + 45$	Add 27 and 173
245	Add 200 and 45

[A] Associative Property of Addition
    Symmetric Property

[B] Commutative Property of Addition
    Associative Property of Addition

[C] Substitution Property
    Transitive Property

[D] Commutative Property of Addition
    Distributive Property

[2.5.2.46] *Dynamic Item*

46. Use the Commutative and Associative Properties to simplify: $\dfrac{2}{5} + \dfrac{1}{3} + 2\dfrac{3}{5} + \dfrac{2}{3}$

[A] $3\dfrac{3}{5}$ [B] 3   [C] 4   [D] $3\dfrac{14}{15}$

Lesson 5: Properties and Mental Computation

[2.5.2.47] *Dynamic Item*

47. Complete each step and name the property used to find the value of $(5 \times 18) \times 2$.

$(18 \times 5) \times 2$	
$18 \times (5 \times 2)$	
	Multiply 5 and 2
	Multiply 18 and 10

[2.5.2.48] *Dynamic Item*

48. Use the Distributive Property to find 5×24. Show each step.

Lesson 6: Adding and Subtracting Expressions

Objective 1: Use the Distributive Property to combine like terms.

[2.6.1.49] *Dynamic Item*

49. Simplify the expression.
$(5x - 5.3) + (2x - 4)$

[A] $7x - 9.3$ [B] $7x + 9.3$ [C] $7x - 1.3$ [D] $4x + 1.3$

[2.6.1.50] *Dynamic Item*

50. Simplify the expression. [A] $8x + 7$ [B] $-3x - 7$ [C] $-3x + 7$ [D] $-3x - 3$
$(2x - 5) - (5x - 2)$

[2.6.1.51] *Dynamic Item*

51. Simplify the expression.
$4x + (2x - 6)$

Lesson 6: Adding and Subtracting Expressions

[2.6.1.52] *Dynamic Item*

52. Use the Distributive Property to show that the following is a true statement.
$11m - 5m = 6m$

Objective 2: Simplify expressions with several variables.

[2.6.2.53] *Dynamic Item*

53. Simplify the expression.
$(3x - 2y) - (7x - 5y)$

   [A] $10x - 7y$ [B] $-4x - 7y$ [C] $10x + 3y$ [D] $-4x + 3y$

[2.6.2.54] *Dynamic Item*

54. Simplify the expression.   [A] $-\dfrac{7}{5}x + 1$ [B] $\dfrac{7}{5}x - 1$ [C] $-\dfrac{7}{5}x - 1$ [D] $\dfrac{7}{5}x + 1$
$\left(\dfrac{3}{5}x - \dfrac{1}{2}\right) + \left(\dfrac{4}{5}x + \dfrac{3}{2}\right)$

[2.6.2.55] *Dynamic Item*

55. Simplify the expression.
$(4.7a + 3.9b) + (6.3a - 6.5b)$

[2.6.2.56] *Dynamic Item*

56. Find an expression in simplest form for the perimeter of the figure.

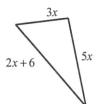

$3x$

$2x + 6$

$5x$

Lesson 7: Multiplying and Dividing Expressions

Objective 1: Multiply expressions containing variables.

[2.7.1.57] *Dynamic Item*

57. Simplify the expression. Use the Distributive Property if needed.
    $(2t)(-5)$

    [A] $-3t$ [B] $10t$ [C] -10 [D] $-10t$

[2.7.1.58] *Dynamic Item*

58. Simplify the expression. Use the Distributive Property if needed.
    $5(9x-2)$

    [A] $45x+10$ [B] $45x+2$ [C] $45x-10$ [D] $45x-2$

[2.7.1.59] *Dynamic Item*

59. Simplify the expression. Use the Distributive Property if needed.
    $4x \cdot 3 - 6x \cdot 4$

[2.7.1.60] *Dynamic Item*

60. What is the area of this rectangle?

$7x$ cm

$12x$ cm

Lesson 7: Multiplying and Dividing Expressions

Objective 2: Divide expressions containing variables.

[2.7.2.61] *Dynamic Item*

61. Simplify the expression. Use the Distributive Property if needed.

$$\frac{24x}{-6}$$

    [A] $-4x$ [B] $18x$ [C] $-x$ [D] -4

[2.7.2.62] *Dynamic Item*

62. Simplify the expression. Use the Distributive Property if needed.

$$\frac{-7+35c}{-7}$$

    [A] $1+35c$ [B] $1+5c$ [C] $1-5c$ [D] $-4c$

[2.7.2.63] *Dynamic Item*

63. Simplify the expression. Use the Distributive Property if needed.

$$\frac{21y+12}{3}$$

[2.7.2.64] *Dynamic Item*

64. Simplify the expression. Use the Distributive Property if needed.

$$\frac{5x^2-15x-75}{5}$$

Lesson 1: The Real Numbers and Absolute Value

Objective 1: Compare real numbers.

[2.1.1.1] *Dynamic Item*

[1] [A]

[2.1.1.2] *Dynamic Item*

[2] [B]

[2.1.1.3] *Dynamic Item*

[3] $-2.47, -\dfrac{6}{5}, \dfrac{5}{8}, 20$

[2.1.1.4] *Dynamic Item*

[4] Answers may vary. One possible answer is $-\dfrac{11}{12}$.

Objective 2: Simplify expressions involving opposites and absolute value.

[2.1.2.5] *Dynamic Item*

[5] [A]

[2.1.2.6] *Dynamic Item*

[6] [A]

[2.1.2.7] *Dynamic Item*

[7] 25

[2.1.2.8] *Dynamic Item*

[8] –2

Lesson 2: Adding Real Numbers

Objective 1: Use algebra tiles to model addition.

[2.2.1.9] *Dynamic Item*

[9] [A]

[2.2.1.10 *Dynamic Item*

[10] [D]

[2.2.1.11] *Dynamic Item*

[11]

[2.2.1.12] *Dynamic Item*

[12] Answers will vary. The total of the black algebra tiles and white algebra tiles must represent 4.

Objective 2: Add numbers with like signs.

[2.2.2.13] *Dynamic Item*

[13] [B]

[2.2.2.14] *Dynamic Item*

[14] [C]

[2.2.2.15] *Dynamic Item*

[15] −9.95

[2.2.2.16] *Dynamic Item*

[16] −16.6

Objective 3: Add numbers with unlike signs.

[2.2.3.17] *Dynamic Item*

[17] [A]

[2.2.3.18] *Dynamic Item*

[18] [B]

[2.2.3.19] *Dynamic Item*

[19] $-2\dfrac{13}{28}$

[2.2.3.20] *Dynamic Item*

[20] 21.5

Lesson 3: Subtracting Real Numbers

Objective 1: Use algebra tiles to model subtraction.

[2.3.1.21] *Dynamic Item*

[21] [B]

[2.3.1.22] *Dynamic Item*

[22] [C]

[2.3.1.23] *Dynamic Item*

[23]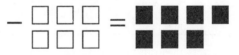

[2.3.1.24] *Dynamic Item*

[24]

Objective 2: Define subtraction in terms of addition.

[2.3.2.25] *Dynamic Item*

[25] [D]

[2.3.2.26] *Dynamic Item*

[26] [D]

[2.3.2.27] *Dynamic Item*

[27] $7+(-6)$

[2.3.2.28] *Dynamic Item*

[28] $12+13+10$

Objective 3: Subtract numbers with like and unlike signs.

[2.3.3.29] *Dynamic Item*

[29] [C]

[2.3.3.30] *Dynamic Item*

[30] [B]

[2.3.3.31] *Dynamic Item*

[31] -17

[2.3.3.32] *Dynamic Item*

[32] 12.7

Lesson 4: Multiplying and Dividing Real Numbers

Objective 1: Multiply and divide positive and negative numbers.

[2.4.1.33] *Dynamic Item*

[33] [C]

[2.4.1.34] *Dynamic Item*

[34] [C]

[2.4.1.35] *Dynamic Item*

[35] $-\dfrac{4}{49}$

[2.4.1.36] *Dynamic Item*

[36] $\dfrac{7}{2}$

Objective 2: Define the Properties of Zero.

[2.4.2.37] *Dynamic Item*

[37] [C]

[2.4.2.38] *Dynamic Item*

[38] [C]

[2.4.2.39] *Dynamic Item*

[39] undefined

[2.4.2.40] *Dynamic Item*

[40]   True. $0 \div 1 = 0$ because $0 \times 1 = 0$.

Lesson 5: Properties and Mental Computation

Objective 1: State and apply the Commutative, Associative, and Distributive Properties.

[2.5.1.41] *Dynamic Item*

[41]   [B]

[2.5.1.42] *Dynamic Item*

[42]   [D]

[2.5.1.43] *Dynamic Item*

$$(17 + 74) + 43 =$$
$$(74 + 17) + 43 = \quad \text{(Commutative Property of Addition)}$$
$$74 + (17 + 43) = \quad \text{(Associative Property of Addition)}$$
$$74 + (60) =$$

[43]   134

[2.5.1.44] *Dynamic Item*

[44] $7b(7c - d)$

Objective 2: Use the Commutative, Associative, and Distributive Properties to perform mental computation.

[2.5.2.45] *Dynamic Item*

[45]   [B]

[2.5.2.46] *Dynamic Item*

[46]   [C]

[2.5.2.47] *Dynamic Item*

$(18 \times 5) \times 2$	Commutative Property of Multiplication
$18 \times (5 \times 2)$	Associative Property of Multiplication
18×10	Multiply 5 and 2
180	Multiply 18 and 10

[47]

[2.5.2.48] *Dynamic Item*

$$5 \times 24 = 5 \times (20 + 4)$$
$$= (5 \times 20) + (5 \times 4)$$
$$= 100 + 20$$
$$= 120$$

[48]

Lesson 6: Adding and Subtracting Expressions

Objective 1: Use the Distributive Property to combine like terms.

[2.6.1.49] *Dynamic Item*

[49] [A]

[2.6.1.50] *Dynamic Item*

[50] [D]

[2.6.1.51] *Dynamic Item*

[51] $6x - 6$

[2.6.1.52] *Dynamic Item*

[52] $11m - 5m = (11 - 5)m = 6m$

Objective 2: Simplify expressions with several variables.

[2.6.2.53] *Dynamic Item*

[53] [D]

[2.6.2.54] *Dynamic Item*

[54] [D]

[2.6.2.55] *Dynamic Item*

[55] $11a - 2.6b$

[2.6.2.56] *Dynamic Item*

[56] $10x + 6$

Lesson 7: Multiplying and Dividing Expressions

Objective 1: Multiply expressions containing variables.

[2.7.1.57] *Dynamic Item*

[57] [D]

[2.7.1.58] *Dynamic Item*

[58] [C]

[2.7.1.59] *Dynamic Item*

[59] $-12x$

[2.7.1.60] *Dynamic Item*

[60] $84x^2$ square centimeters

Algebra 1

Objective 2: Divide expressions containing variables.

[2.7.2.61] *Dynamic Item*

[61] [A]

[2.7.2.62] *Dynamic Item*

[62] [C]

[2.7.2.63] *Dynamic Item*

[63] $7y + 4$

[2.7.2.64] *Dynamic Item*

[64] $x^2 - 3x - 15$

Lesson 1: Solving Equations by Adding and Subtracting

Objective 1: Solve equations by using addition and subtraction.

[3.1.1.1] *Dynamic Item*

1. Solve the equation.
   $x - 5.2 = 6.8$

   [A] 12　　　　[B] 1.6　　　　[C] –1.6　　　　[D] –12

[3.1.1.2] *Dynamic Item*

2. Solve the equation.
   $x - \dfrac{1}{7} = \dfrac{2}{3}$

   [A] $\dfrac{34}{7}$　　[B] $\dfrac{17}{3}$　　[C] $\dfrac{5}{42}$　　[D] $\dfrac{17}{21}$

[3.1.1.3] *Dynamic Item*

3. Solve the equation.
   $-55 = 27 - m$

[3.1.1.4] *Dynamic Item*

4. Write and solve an equation to find the measure of the third angle of a triangle with two angles measuring 58° and 23°. The sum of the angles of a triangle is 180°.

Lesson 2: Solving Equations by Multiplying and Dividing

Objective 1: Solve equations by using multiplication and division.

[3.2.1.5] *Dynamic Item*

5. Solve the equation.
   $29 = -7y$

   [A] $-\dfrac{29}{7}$　　[B] –36　　[C] $\dfrac{29}{7}$　　[D] 36

[3.2.1.6] *Dynamic Item*

6. Solve the equation.
   $-\dfrac{4}{5}x = -7$

   [A] $\dfrac{35}{4}$　　[B] $\dfrac{20}{7}$　　[C] $\dfrac{1}{7}$　　[D] –3

Lesson 2: Solving Equations by Multiplying and Dividing

[3.2.1.7] *Dynamic Item*

7. Solve the equation.

$$6.86 = \frac{z}{0.03}$$

[3.2.1.8] *Dynamic Item*

8. At the Last Chance Filling Station, gas costs $1.98 a gallon. Sophia paid $29.70 to fill her tank. Write and solve an equation to find the number of gallons Sophia bought.

Lesson 3: Solving Two-Step Equations

Objective 1: Write equations that represent real-world situations.

[3.3.1.9] *Dynamic Item*

9. Hans pays $384 in advance on his account at the athletic club. Each time he uses the club, $6 is deducted from the account. Write an equation that represents the value remaining in his account after x visits to the club. Find the value remaining in the account after 11 visits.

[A] $V = 384 - 6x$; $2315   [B] $V = 384 - 6x$; $2301

[C] $V = 6 - 384x$; $318   [D] $V = 384 - 6x$; $318

[3.3.1.10] *Dynamic Item*

10. The Starlight Tree Farm sells Douglas firs and noble firs. One December they sold 178 more Douglas firs than noble firs. The total number of trees sold was 578. Which equation could be used to solve for n, the number of noble fir trees sold?

[A] $n - 178 = 578$ [B] $n + 178 = 578$ [C] $2n - 178 = 578$ [D] $2n + 178 = 578$

[3.3.1.11] *Dynamic Item*

11. The ecology club is selling calendars to raise money. The supplier charges a one-time fee of $55 for each order and $2 for each calendar. Write and solve an equation for the number of calendars the ecology club can purchase if their budget is $475.

Lesson 3: Solving Two-Step Equations

[3.3.1.12] *Dynamic Item*

12. A rental car agency charges $13 per day plus 17 cents per mile to rent a certain car. Write and solve an equation to find the number of miles driven if the car was rented for 3 days and the total bill was $95.95.

Objective 2: Solve two-step equations.

[3.3.2.13] *Dynamic Item*

13. Solve the equation.   [A] −5   [B] 6   [C] 35   [D] 4

$$-3 = -4 - \frac{x}{5}$$

[3.3.2.14] *Dynamic Item*

14. Solve the equation.   [A] −1.19   [B] −0.56   [C] 4.06   [D] 2.50
$-1.6x - 3.7 = -2.8$

[3.3.2.15] *Dynamic Item*

15. Solve the equation.

$$5.6 = 4.2 + \frac{x}{4}$$

[3.3.2.16] *Dynamic Item*

16. Solve the equation.
$-5 + 5x = 10$

Lesson 4: Solving Multistep Equations

Objective 1: Write and solve multistep equations.

[3.4.1.17] *Dynamic Item*

17. Solve the equation.   [A] $\frac{1}{4}$ [B] $-\frac{3}{4}$ [C] $-\frac{3}{10}$ [D] $-1\frac{1}{3}$
$7x + 2 = 3x - 1$

Lesson 4: Solving Multistep Equations

[3.4.1.18] *Dynamic Item*

18. Solve the equation.   [A] 2.54   [B] 0.39   [C] 3.42   [D] 0.61
$$-5.8x - 1.1 = 4.6x - 5.2$$

[3.4.1.19] *Dynamic Item*

19. Solve the equation.
$$5x + \frac{3}{8} - 3x - \frac{5}{8} = \frac{5}{8}$$

[3.4.1.20] *Dynamic Item*

20. One side of an equilateral triangle increased by 19 is 31 less than three times another side. If the sides are measured in inches, what are the measures of the three sides of the triangle?

Lesson 5: Using the Distributive Property

Objective 1: Use the Distributive Property to solve equations.

[3.5.1.21] *Dynamic Item*

21. Solve the equation.   [A] 6   [B] 11   [C] 13   [D] 8
$$2 = 2(x - 5) + 1 - x$$

[3.5.1.22] *Dynamic Item*

22. Solve the equation.   [A] 0   [B] 1   [C] all real numbers   [D] no solution
$$2(x + 3) = -2(-1 - 3x)$$

[3.5.1.23] *Dynamic Item*

23. Solve the equation.
$$2(4x - 5) = x + 2$$

Lesson 5: Using the Distributive Property

[3.5.1.24] *Dynamic Item*

24. Solve the equation.
$$(x-2) + 5 = 2(x+1) + 1$$

Objective 2: Solve real-world problems by using multistep equations.

[3.5.2.25] *Dynamic Item*

25. How many degrees are in angle *H*? The sum of the angle measures of a triangle is 180°.

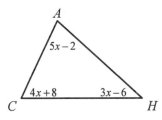

    [A] 18°   [B] 15°   [C] 14°   [D] 12°

[3.5.2.26] *Dynamic Item*

26. You sell computers and earn a $30,000 salary, plus a bonus. Your bonus is $\frac{1}{40}$ of the amount by which your sales exceed $400,000. Which must your sales be in order for you to earn a total of $60,000?

    [A] $2,830,000   [B] $10,750   [C] $1,700,000   [D] $1,600,000

[3.5.2.27] *Dynamic Item*

27. The perimeter of a triangle is 59 centimeters. Side *b* is 4 centimeters longer than side *a*. Side *c* is 5 centimeters shorter than twice the length of side *a*. Find the length of each side.

[3.5.2.28] *Dynamic Item*

28. The perimeter of a rectangle is $P = 2L + 2W$, where *L* is the length and *W* is the width. If the perimeter is 140 feet and the length is 10 feet more than the width, what are the dimensions?

Lesson 6: Using Formulas and Literal Equations

Objective 1: Solve literal equations for a specific variable.

[3.6.1.29] *Dynamic Item*

29. Solve the equation for the indicated variable.
$B = 5y$, for y

   [A] $y = 5 - B$ [B] $y = B - 5$ [C] $y = \dfrac{5}{B}$ [D] $y = \dfrac{B}{5}$

[3.6.1.30] *Dynamic Item*

30. Solve the equation for the indicated variable.
$U = mgh$, for h

   [A] $h = U + mg$ [B] $h = \dfrac{mg}{U}$ [C] $h = U - mg$ [D] $h = \dfrac{U}{mg}$

[3.6.1.31] *Dynamic Item*

31. Solve the equation for the indicated variable.
$3 = t - 7s$, for t

[3.6.1.32] *Dynamic Item*

32. Solve the equation for the indicated variable.
$11p - 3q = -4$, for p

Objective 2: Use formulas to solve problems.

[3.6.2.33] *Dynamic Item*

33. Use the formula $C = \dfrac{5}{9}(F - 32)$ to convert $68°\,F$ to degrees Celsius.

   [A] $36°\,C$ [B] $6°\,C$ [C] $180°\,C$ [D] $20°\,C$

Lesson 6: Using Formulas and Literal Equations

[3.6.2.34] *Dynamic Item*

34. Use the formula $C = 2\pi r$ to find the radius, r, for a circle with a circumference of 185 centimeters. Round your answer to the nearest hundredth.

   [A] 25.56 cm   [B] 29.46 cm   [C] 58.92 cm   [D] 92.50 cm

[3.6.2.35] *Dynamic Item*

35. A public storage company charges new customers an initial fee of $20.00. Each month of storage costs $16.50. The company wrote the following formula to calculate the total charges: $T = 20.00 + 16.50m$, where T is the total charges, and m is the number of months of storage. How many months could a customer rent storage space for $300.50?

[3.6.2.36] *Dynamic Item*

36. Use the formula $A = \dfrac{1}{2}h(a+b)$ to find the length of the missing base for a trapezoid with $A = 84$ cm^2, base $a = 5$ cm, and height $h = 7$ cm.

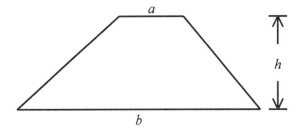

Lesson 1: Solving Equations by Adding and Subtracting

Objective 1: Solve equations by using addition and subtraction.

[3.1.1.1] *Dynamic Item*

[1] [A]

[3.1.1.2] *Dynamic Item*

[2] [D]

[3.1.1.3] *Dynamic Item*

[3] 82

[3.1.1.4] *Dynamic Item*

[4] $x + 58 + 23 = 180;\ 99°$

Lesson 2: Solving Equations by Multiplying and Dividing

Objective 1: Solve equations by using multiplication and division.

[3.2.1.5] *Dynamic Item*

[5] [A]

[3.2.1.6] *Dynamic Item*

[6] [A]

[3.2.1.7] *Dynamic Item*

[7] 0.2058

[3.2.1.8] *Dynamic Item*

[8] $1.98g = 29.70;\ g = 15$

Lesson 3: Solving Two-Step Equations

Objective 1: Write equations that represent real-world situations.

[3.3.1.9] *Dynamic Item*

[9] [D]

[3.3.1.10] *Dynamic Item*

[10] [D]

[3.3.1.11] *Dynamic Item*

[11] $2n + 55 = 475;\ 210$ calendars

[3.3.1.12] *Dynamic Item*

$(13)(3) + 0.17m = 95.95$

[12] 335 miles

Objective 2: Solve two-step equations.

[3.3.2.13] *Dynamic Item*

[13] [A]

[3.3.2.14] *Dynamic Item*

[14] [B]

[3.3.2.15] *Dynamic Item*

[15] 5.6

[3.3.2.16] *Dynamic Item*

[16] $x = 3$

Lesson 4: Solving Multistep Equations

Objective 1: Write and solve multistep equations.

[3.4.1.17] *Dynamic Item*

[17] [B]

[3.4.1.18] *Dynamic Item*

[18] [B]

[3.4.1.19] *Dynamic Item*

[19] $\dfrac{7}{16}$

[3.4.1.20] *Dynamic Item*

[20] 25 inches

Lesson 5: Using the Distributive Property

Objective 1: Use the Distributive Property to solve equations.

[3.5.1.21] *Dynamic Item*

[21] [B]

[3.5.1.22] *Dynamic Item*

[22] [B]

[3.5.1.23] *Dynamic Item*

[23] $\dfrac{12}{7}$

[3.5.1.24] *Dynamic Item*

[24] $x = 0$

Objective 2: Solve real-world problems by using multistep equations.

[3.5.2.25] *Dynamic Item*

[25] [B]

[3.5.2.26] *Dynamic Item*

[26] [D]

[3.5.2.27] *Dynamic Item*

[27] side $a = 15$ cm; side $b = 19$ cm; side $c = 25$ cm

[3.5.2.28] *Dynamic Item*

[28] 30 ft by 40 ft

Lesson 6: Using Formulas and Literal Equations

Objective 1: Solve literal equations for a specific variable.

[3.6.1.29] *Dynamic Item*

[29] [D]

[3.6.1.30] *Dynamic Item*

[30] [D]

[3.6.1.31] *Dynamic Item*

[31] $t = 3 + 7s$

[3.6.1.32] *Dynamic Item*

[32] $p = \dfrac{-4 + 3q}{11}$

Objective 2: Use formulas to solve problems.

[3.6.2.33] *Dynamic Item*

[33] [D]

[3.6.2.34] *Dynamic Item*

[34] [B]

[3.6.2.35] *Dynamic Item*

[35] 17 months

[3.6.2.36] *Dynamic Item*

[36] 19 cm

Lesson 1: Using Proportional Reasoning

Objective 1: Identify the means and extremes of a proportion.

[4.1.1.1] *Dynamic Item*

1. Which of the following proportions is *not* true?

[A] $\frac{3}{7} \overset{?}{=} \frac{9}{21}$ [B] $\frac{3}{7} \overset{?}{=} \frac{12}{28}$ [C] $\frac{27}{63} \overset{?}{=} \frac{3}{7}$ [D] $\frac{3}{7} \overset{?}{=} \frac{9}{28}$

[4.1.1.2] *Dynamic Item*

2. Which are the means of the proportion?

$$\frac{q}{r} = \frac{s}{t}$$

[A] q and r [B] r and t [C] q and t [D] r and s

[4.1.1.3] *Dynamic Item*

3. What is the cross product that could be used to determine if these ratios are equal?

$$\frac{16}{19} \text{ and } \frac{128}{190}$$

[4.1.1.4] *Dynamic Item*

4. Is $\frac{0.4}{1.3} = \frac{1.6}{5.2}$ a true proportion? Explain.

Objective 2: Use proportions to solve problems.

[4.1.2.5] *Dynamic Item*

5. If Kioko can run 4 miles in 32 minutes, how long will it take him to run 6 miles at this rate?

[A] 40 minutes   [B] 56 minutes   [C] 32 minutes   [D] 48 minutes

Lesson 1: Using Proportional Reasoning

[4.1.2.6] *Dynamic Item*

6. Solve the proportion. Round to the nearest hundredth if necessary.

$$\frac{5}{6} = \frac{d}{18}$$

[A] 3   [B] 30   [C] 15   [D] 17

[4.1.2.7] *Dynamic Item*

7. Solve the proportion. Round to the nearest hundredth if necessary.

$$\frac{0.7}{14} = \frac{0.04}{n}$$

[4.1.2.8] *Dynamic Item*

8. The triangles below are similar. Find x.

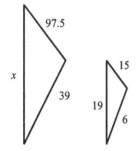

Lesson 2: Percent Problems

Objective 1: Find equivalent fractions, decimals, and percents.

[4.2.1.9] *Dynamic Item*

9. Which is 1% written as a decimal?   [A] 0.001   [B] 0.1   [C] 0.0001   [D] 0.01

Lesson 2: Percent Problems

[4.2.1.10] *Dynamic Item*

10. Which is 27% written as a fraction?   [A] $2\frac{7}{10}$ [B] $3\frac{19}{27}$ [C] 27   [D] $\frac{27}{100}$

[4.2.1.11] *Dynamic Item*

11. Write 0.35 as a percent.

[4.2.1.12] *Dynamic Item*

12. Write $1\frac{19}{20}$ as a percent.

Objective 2: Solve problems involving percent.

[4.2.2.13] *Dynamic Item*

13. Find 50% of 60.   [A] 30   [B] 45   [C] 40   [D] 28

[4.2.2.14] *Dynamic Item*

14. What percent of 128 is 48?   [A] 8%   [B] $37\frac{1}{2}$%   [C] 38%   [D] $\frac{3}{8}$%

[4.2.2.15] *Dynamic Item*

15. 18 is 50% of what number?

[4.2.2.16] *Dynamic Item*

16. In 2000 the circulation of a local newspaper was 11,200. In 2001 its circulation was 11,760. What percent increase is this?

Lesson 3: Introduction to Probability

Objective 1: Find the experimental probability that an event will occur.

[4.3.1.17] *Dynamic Item*

17. Andy and Beth tossed a coin 50 times and got heads 26 times. To the nearest whole percent, what is the experimental probability of tossing a head using Andy and Beth's results?

    [A]   34%   [B]   52%   [C]   48%   [D]   32%

[4.3.1.18] *Dynamic Item*

18. At the Rockville Middle School carnival, 16 of the first 140 people who played the ring toss game won the first prize, 32 won the second prize, and 48 won the third prize. What is the experimental probability of not winning the first, second, or third prize?

    [A]   31%   [B]   32%   [C]   69%   [D]   57%

[4.3.1.19] *Dynamic Item*

19. Jamila spins a spinner like the one below 40 times. It lands on 3 six times. To the nearest hundredth, what is the experimental probability of spinning a 3?

[4.3.1.20] *Dynamic Item*

20. A six-sided number cube is rolled 60 times. Two comes up 7 times. To the nearest hundredth, what is the experimental probability of rolling a two?

Lesson 4: Measures of Central Tendency

Objective 1: Find the mean, median, mode, and range of a data set.

[4.4.1.21] *Dynamic Item*

21. The high temperature for Aug. 15 during the past 10 years is given in the table below.

TEMPERATURE RECORD

Year	Temperature
1988	90° F
1989	90° F
1990	86° F
1991	78° F
1992	79° F
1993	84° F
1994	85° F
1995	90° F
1996	85° F
1997	78° F

What is the mode of these temperatures?

[A] 90°F   [B] 89.9°F   [C] 84.5°F   [D] 85°F

[4.4.1.22] *Dynamic Item*

22. Mike was in charge of collecting contributions for the Food Bank. He received contributions of $100, $80, $90, $110, $100. The next potential contributor wanted to give an amount in line with the other contributions, so he asked, "What is an acceptable amount to give?" Mike decided to use the median value as his answer. Which is the median?

[A] $30   [B] $110   [C] $96   [D] $100

Lesson 4: Measures of Central Tendency

[4.4.1.23] *Dynamic Item*

23. This is a table of scores on a quiz:

Name	Score
Cindy	3
Bob	2
Wendy	3
Max	5
Sarah	5
Frank	8

a. Find the median and mean for these scores.
b. If Bob and Frank each scored one more point, and Cindy and Wendy each scored one fewer, find the new median and mean.

[4.4.1.24] *Dynamic Item*

24. The doctor has asked that Tai's temperature be recorded every 2 hours. Starting at 6 A.M., her mother records the following temperatures: 100.9° F, 102.4° F, 100.7° F, 101.4° F, 100.8° F, and 100.3° F. What is the range of Tai's temperatures?

Objective 2: Represent data with frequency tables.

[4.4.2.25] *Dynamic Item*

25. Clarissa is on the speech team at Baker High School. She has won the ribbons shown on the tally chart at her speech meets this year. What is her median place of finish?

Place	Number of Times
First	ЖЖ ||||
Second	ЖЖ
Third	ЖЖ |||
Fourth	ЖЖ

[A] Between Second and Third   [B] Third

[C] Between Third and Fourth   [D] Second

Lesson 4: Measures of Central Tendency

[4.4.2.26] *Dynamic Item*

26. Which is the mean price per item for the following catalog items?

Price	Frequency
$11	|||||
$14	||
$17	||||| ||
$20	|||

   [A] $16.38　　　　[B] $15.50　　　　[C] $15.41　　　　[D] $65.50

[4.4.2.27] *Dynamic Item*

27. Make a frequency table for the following data which shows the retirement ages of males at a local insurance company.
59, 81, 77, 64, 60, 75, 61, 57, 72, 78, 66, 59, 60, 72, 84, 68, 66, 71, 79, 81

[4.4.2.28] *Dynamic Item*

28. Here are the results of last week's spelling test in Ms. Nkrumah's morning classes. The tally chart shows the number of students who got a given number of words right on the test.

Number Answered Correctly out of 10 questions	
4						
5										
6												
7	
8								
9			
10					

What is the mean number of words the students got correct? Round to the nearest tenth.

Lesson 5: Graphing Data

Objective 1: Interpret line graphs, bar graphs, and circle graphs.

[4.5.1.29] *Dynamic Item*

29. The line graph below shows the amounts of Gennifer's phone bill from May through August in 1996 and 1997.

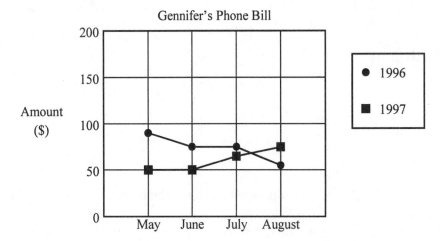

About how much more was Gennifer's phone bill in May 1996 than in May 1997?

[A] $60   [B] $90   [C] $20   [D] $40

Lesson 5: Graphing Data

[4.5.1.30] *Dynamic Item*

30. This bar graph shows how many bottles of each kind of shampoo were sold at Pic'n'Go in one month.

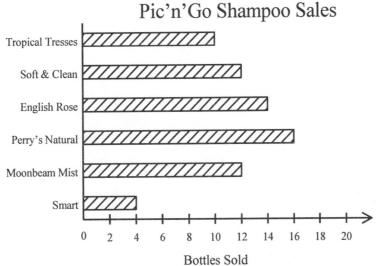

Smart and English Rose are both made by Biggs Company. Tropical Tresses and Perry's Natural are both made by MegaCorp. Which company sold more shampoo at Pic'n'Go? How much more?

[A] Biggs Company, 18 bottles

[B] MegaCorp, 8 bottles

[C] Biggs Company, 8 bottles

[D] MegaCorp, 26 bottles

Lesson 5: Graphing Data

[4.5.1.31] *Dynamic Item*

31. The number of registrations by breed in the Clover City Kennel Club is summarized in the following circle graph. If there were about 3,000 total registrations, about how many Labrador retrievers were registered?

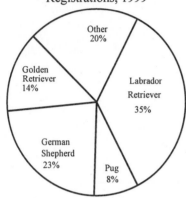

Clover City Kennel Club
Registrations, 1999

Lesson 5: Graphing Data

[4.5.1.32] *Dynamic Item*

32. The bar graph shows the average life spans of several animals.

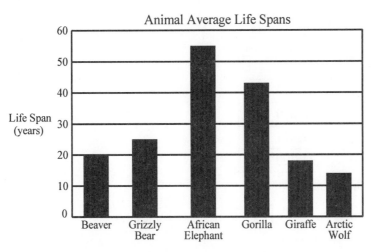

a. Which animal has the longest average life span?
b. What is the average life span of an arctic wolf?
c. About how many years longer is the average life span of an African elephant than the average life span of a beaver?

Objective 2: Represent data with circle graphs.

[4.5.2.33] *Dynamic Item*

33. The table shows the percent of U.S. car sales by vehicle type in 1995.

U.S. Car Sales, 1995

Type	Percent
Small	24
Midsize	33
Large	8
Luxury	35

If a circle graph is made for this data, how many degrees should be used for midsize cars?

[A] 118.8°   [B] 123.8°   [C] 115.8°   [D] 125.8°

Lesson 5: Graphing Data

[4.5.2.34] *Dynamic Item*

34. The table below shows the amount of money on loan to U.S. farmers in 1986, categorized by type of lender.

Lenders	Amount Loaned (in millions of dollars)
Federal land banks	37,660
FMHA	10,349
Life insurance companies	10,940
Commercial banks	12,711
Other	24,000

Which is a circle graph of these data?

▨ Federal land banks   ■ FMHA   ☐ Life insurance companies
⊟ Commercial banks   ▥ Other

[A]

[B]

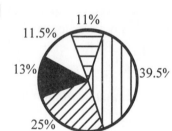

[C]

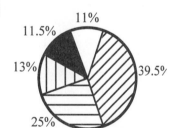

[D]

Lesson 5: Graphing Data

[4.5.2.35] *Dynamic Item*

35. Theo made the following table to show the number of middle school students who attended the last football game.

Grade	Number of Students Attending Game
6	375
7	525
8	100

If this data were displayed in a circle graph, what percent of the graph would show the number of sixth graders who attended the game?

[4.5.2.36] *Dynamic Item*

36. Listed below is the percentage of students registered for various majors at college. Use this information to make a circle graph.

Business   30%

Engineering   15%

Liberal Arts   25%

Undecided   30%

Lesson 5: Graphing Data

Objective 3: Analyze graphs in order to find a misleading presentation of data.

[4.5.3.37] *Dynamic Item*

37. Both graphs represent the number of new clients signed up each month at Superior Realty. Which statement is true?

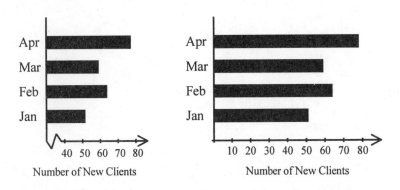

[A] The second graph distorts the relative lengths of the bars on the graph.

[B] The scales on the two graphs are exactly the same.

[C] The two graphs use different data.

[D] none of these

Lesson 5: Graphing Data

[4.5.3.38] *Dynamic Item*

38. Both graphs represent the average number of rentals each day of the year at Happydays Videos. Which statement is true?

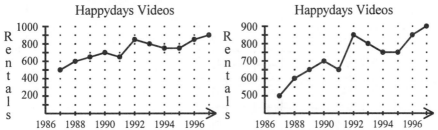

[A] The second graph shows greater changes in the number of rentals than first graph.

[B] The second graph exaggerates the difference in sales each year.

[C] The second graph does not exaggerate the high points on the graph.

[D] none of these

[4.5.3.39] *Dynamic Item*

39. The graph below shows the number of students receiving A's within each grade level at a middle school. Tell why this graph is misleading.

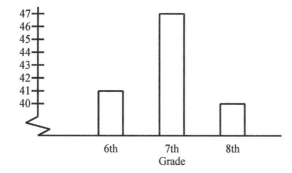

Lesson 5: Graphing Data

[4.5.3.40] *Dynamic Item*

40. An electric company sent out a graph to compare kilowatt hours for the years 1994 and 1995. The graphs below show the usage for a particular household for the two years.

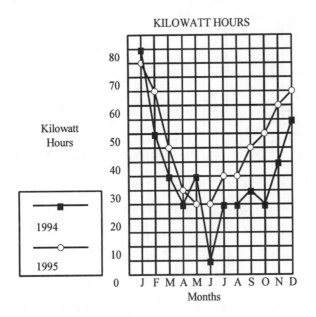

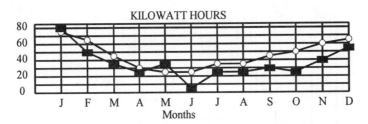

a. Describe how the two graphs are different.

b. Which graph would you use to persuade people there was very little change in kilowatt usage for the two years?

Lesson 6: Other Data Displays

Objective 1: Interpret stem-and-leaf plots, histograms, and box-and-whisker plots.

[4.6.1.41] *Dynamic Item*

41. What is the smallest number shown on the stem-and-leaf plot below?

Stem	Leaf
0	4 7
1	1 2 4
2	1 4 4
3	3 5
4	2 6

$1 | 0 = 10$

[A] 1   [B] 40   [C] 11   [D] 4

[4.6.1.42] *Dynamic Item*

42. The test scores for the 31 members of a math class are represented in the histogram. How many students had scores between 110 and 119?

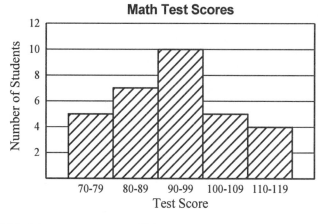

Math Test Scores

[A] 14   [B] 5   [C] 4   [D] 9

Lesson 6: Other Data Displays

[4.6.1.43] *Dynamic Item*

43. The histogram shows the number of minutes students at Montrose Junior High typically spend on household chores each day. About how many students spend 61-80 minutes on chores?

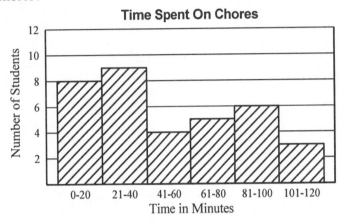

[4.6.1.44] *Dynamic Item*

44. What is the median of the data shown in the box-and-whisker plot below?

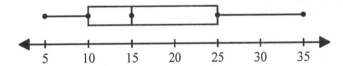

Lesson 6: Other Data Displays

Objective 2: Represent data with stem-and-leaf plots, histograms, and box-and-whisker plots.

[4.6.2.45] *Dynamic Item*

45. Make a stem-and-leaf plot for the following data.
60, 65, 76, 70, 86, 90, 85, 71, 94, 96, 77, 93, 98, 81, 67

[A]
Stem	Leaf
6	0 5 7
7	0 1 6 7 5
8	1 6
9	0 3 4 6 8

6 | 4 = 64

[B]
Stem	Leaf
6	0 5 7
7	0 1 6 7
8	1 5 6
9	0 3 4 6 8

6 | 4 = 64

[C]
Stem	Leaf
60	0 5 7
70	0 1 6 7
80	1 5 6
90	0 3 4 6 8

60 | 4 = 64

[D]
Stem	Leaf
60	0 5 7
70	0 1 6 7 5
80	1 6
90	0 3 4 6 8

60 | 4 = 64

[4.6.2.46] *Dynamic Item*

46. Which set of data is represented by the box-and-whisker plot?

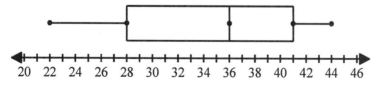

[A] 41, 36, 22, 35, 44, 40, 28   [B] 41, 34, 22, 35, 44, 40, 28

[C] 41, 36, 22, 27, 44, 40, 28   [D] 41, 36, 22, 35, 46, 40, 28

Lesson 6: Other Data Displays

[4.6.2.47] *Dynamic Item*

47. The data below shows the average daily high temperature for Madison, Wisconsin, for each month of the year. Use a stem-and-leaf plot to organize the data.
65, 61, 57, 67, 76, 75, 52, 82, 71, 58, 63, 80

[4.6.2.48] *Dynamic Item*

48. The table below shows the number of days that received rain, measured to the nearest hundredth of an inch, over a three-month period in Carlsville.

Rainfall in inches	0.00 – 0.19	0.20 – 0.39	0.40 - 0.59	0.60 - 0.79	0.80 - 0.99	1.00 - 1.19	1.20 - 1.39	1.40 - up
Number of Days	37	20	12	5	3	4	5	2

Draw a histogram which reflects this data.

Algebra 1
78

Lesson 1: Using Proportional Reasoning

Objective 1: Identify the means and extremes of a proportion.

[4.1.1.1] *Dynamic Item*

[1] [D]

[4.1.1.2] *Dynamic Item*

[2] [D]

[4.1.1.3] *Dynamic Item*

[3] $19 \times 128 \overset{?}{=} 16 \times 190$

[4.1.1.4] *Dynamic Item*

[4] yes; $0.4(5.2) = 1.3(1.6)$

Objective 2: Use proportions to solve problems.

[4.1.2.5] *Dynamic Item*

[5] [D]

[4.1.2.6] *Dynamic Item*

[6] [C]

[4.1.2.7] *Dynamic Item*

[7] $n = 0.8$

[4.1.2.8] *Dynamic Item*

[8] 123.5

Lesson 2: Percent Problems

Objective 1: Find equivalent fractions, decimals, and percents.

[4.2.1.9] *Dynamic Item*

[9] [D]

[4.2.1.10] *Dynamic Item*

[10] [D]

[4.2.1.11] *Dynamic Item*

[11] 35%

[4.2.1.12] *Dynamic Item*

[12] 195%

Objective 2: Solve problems involving percent.

[4.2.2.13] *Dynamic Item*

[13] [A]

[4.2.2.14] *Dynamic Item*

[14] [B]

[4.2.2.15] *Dynamic Item*

[15] 36

[4.2.2.16] *Dynamic Item*

[16] 5%

Lesson 3: Introduction to Probability

Objective 1: Find the experimental probability that an event will occur.

[4.3.1.17] *Dynamic Item*

[17] [B]

[4.3.1.18] *Dynamic Item*

[18] [A]

[4.3.1.19] *Dynamic Item*

[19] 0.15 or 15%

[4.3.1.20] *Dynamic Item*

[20] 0.12 or 12%

Lesson 4: Measures of Central Tendency

Objective 1: Find the mean, median, mode, and range of a data set.

[4.4.1.21] *Dynamic Item*

[21] [A]

[4.4.1.22] *Dynamic Item*

[22] [D]

[4.4.1.23] *Dynamic Item*

a. median is 4
   mean is 4.33333

b. median is 4
[23]   mean is 4.33333

Algebra 1

[4.4.1.24] *Dynamic Item*

[24] 2.1°F

Objective 2: Represent data with frequency tables.

[4.4.2.25] *Dynamic Item*

[25] [D]

[4.4.2.26] *Dynamic Item*

[26] [C]

[4.4.2.27] *Dynamic Item*

50-59	|||
60-69	Ⅲ‖ ||
70-79	Ⅲ‖ ||
80-89	|||

[27]

[4.4.2.28] *Dynamic Item*

[28] 6.4

Lesson 5: Graphing Data

Objective 1: Interpret line graphs, bar graphs, and circle graphs.

[4.5.1.29] *Dynamic Item*

[29] [D]

[4.5.1.30] *Dynamic Item*

[30] [B]

[4.5.1.31] *Dynamic Item*

[31]   1050

[4.5.1.32] *Dynamic Item*

   a. African elephant
   b. 14 years
[32]   c. about 35 years

Objective 2: Represent data with circle graphs.

[4.5.2.33] *Dynamic Item*

[33]   [A]

[4.5.2.34] *Dynamic Item*

[34]   [A]

[4.5.2.35] *Dynamic Item*

[35]   37.5%

[4.5.2.36] *Dynamic Item*

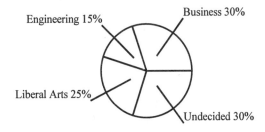

Registration of Various College Majors

Engineering 15%   Business 30%

Liberal Arts 25%

Undecided 30%

[36]

Objective 3: Analyze graphs in order to find a misleading presentation of data.

[4.5.3.37] *Dynamic Item*

[37] [D]

[4.5.3.38] *Dynamic Item*

[38] [B]

[4.5.3.39] *Dynamic Item*

[39] The scale for the graph does not begin at 0. This makes it appear that the 7th grade has many more students with A's than the other classes.

[4.5.3.40] *Dynamic Item*

a. Sample Response: The first graph makes it appear that there were significant changes in the use of electricity over the year, while the second graph makes it appear that there was very little change.
[40] b. second graph

Lesson 6: Other Data Displays

Objective 1: Interpret stem-and-leaf plots, histograms, and box-and-whisker plots.

[4.6.1.41] *Dynamic Item*

[41] [D]

[4.6.1.42] *Dynamic Item*

[42] [C]

[4.6.1.43] *Dynamic Item*

[43] 5 students

[4.6.1.44] *Dynamic Item*

[44] 15

Objective 2: Represent data with stem-and-leaf plots, histograms, and box-and-whisker plots.

[4.6.2.45] *Dynamic Item*

[45] [B]

[4.6.2.46] *Dynamic Item*

[46] [A]

[4.6.2.47] *Dynamic Item*

```
        5 | 2 7 8
        6 | 1 3 5 7
        7 | 1 5 6
[47]    8 | 0 2
```

[4.6.2.48] *Dynamic Item*

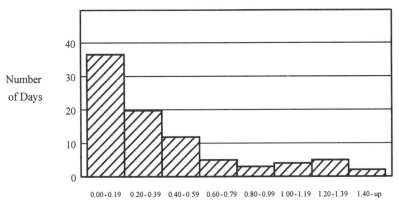

[48] _____

Lesson 1: Linear Functions and Graphs

Objective 1: Determine whether a relation is a function.

[5.1.1.1] *Dynamic Item*

1. Which of the following relations is also a function?

[A]

x	y
–8	6
–7	4
–7	2

[B]

x	y
–7	6
–6	4
–7	2

[C]

x	y
–7	2
–6	–1
–5	–2

[D]

x	y
–6	6
–6	4
–7	2

[5.1.1.2] *Dynamic Item*

2. Complete each ordered pair so that it is a solution for the equation $2x + y = 2$.
   $(\_\_, 0), (0, \_\_), (-1, \_\_), (\_\_, -2)$

   [A] $(1, 0), (0, 2), (-1, -1), (-2, -2)$ [B] $(1, 0), (0, 2), (-1, -2), (-1, -2)$

   [C] $(1, 0), (0, 2), (-1, 4), (2, -2)$ [D] $(0, 1), (2, 0), (4, -1), (-2, 2)$

[5.1.1.3] *Dynamic Item*

3. Find an ordered pair which could be added to this set of ordered pairs so that the relation would not be a function.
   $\{(-4, 3), (5, 3), (2, 3)\}$

[5.1.1.4] *Dynamic Item*

4. Determine whether the relation is a function. Explain.
   $\{(5, 8), (7, 9), (7, 6), (9, 5)\}$

Lesson 1: Linear Functions and Graphs

Objective 2: Describe the domain and range of a function.

[5.1.2.5] *Dynamic Item*

5. Determine the domain and range of the given relation.
   $\{(2, 16), (3, 24), (4, 32), (5, 40)\}$

   [A] Domain: $\{2, 3, 4, 5\}$
       Range: $\{16, 24, 32, 40\}$

   [B] Domain: $\{(4, 32), (5, 40)\}$
       Range: $\{(2, 16), (3, 24)\}$

   [C] Domain: $\{(2, 16), (3, 24)\}$
       Range: $\{(4, 32), (5, 40)\}$

   [D] Domain: $\{16, 24, 32, 40\}$
       Range: $\{2, 3, 4, 5\}$

[5.1.2.6] *Dynamic Item*

6. Determine the domain and range of the given relation if y is a function of x.

x	-7	-6	-2	3	7
y	1	-3	3	2	6

   [A] Domain: $\{1, -3, 3, 2, 6\}$
       Range: $\{1, -3, 3, 2, 6\}$

   [B] Domain: $\{-7, -6, -2, 3, 7\}$
       Range: $\{-7, -6, -2, 3, 7\}$

   [C] Domain: $\{1, -3, 3, 2, 6\}$
       Range: $\{-7, -6, -2, 3, 7\}$

   [D] Domain: $\{-7, -6, -2, 3, 7\}$
       Range: $\{1, -3, 3, 2, 6\}$

[5.1.2.7] *Dynamic Item*

7. Determine the domain and range of the relation.

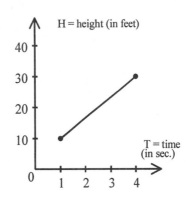

Algebra 1

Lesson 1: Linear Functions and Graphs

[5.1.2.8] *Dynamic Item*

8. Plumber X charges an initial fee of $40 for a home visit with an additional cost of $32 per hour worked. Complete the table of values. Write an equation to show the total cost, C, for Plumber X for n hours worked. Find the domain and range of the function. Assume $n \leq 100$.

Number of hours worked	Total Cost
1	$72
2	
3	
4	
5	

Lesson 2: Defining Slope

Objective 1: Calculate the slope of a line using the rise and run.

[5.2.1.9] *Dynamic Item*

9. Find the slope of the line.

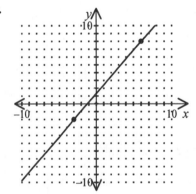

[A] $\dfrac{9}{10}$ [B] $-\dfrac{10}{9}$ [C] $-\dfrac{9}{10}$ [D] $\dfrac{10}{9}$

Lesson 2: Defining Slope

[5.2.1.10] *Dynamic Item*

10. Find the slope for the given rise and run.

rise: 4, run: $4\frac{1}{4}$

[A] $\frac{16}{17}$ [B] $\frac{17}{16}$ [C] $-\frac{16}{17}$ [D] $-\frac{17}{16}$

[5.2.1.11] *Dynamic Item*

11. Find the slope for the given rise and run.
rise: -2, run: 6

[5.2.1.12] *Dynamic Item*

12. Find the slope of the line.

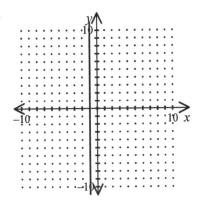

Objective 2: Calculate the slope of a line from the ratio of the differences in x- and y-coordinates.

[5.2.2.13] *Dynamic Item*

13. Find the slope of the line that contains the given pair of points.
(2, 13) and (11, 5)

[A] $-\frac{8}{9}$ [B] $-\frac{9}{8}$ [C] $-\frac{6}{11}$ [D] $-\frac{11}{6}$

Lesson 2: Defining Slope

[5.2.2.14] *Dynamic Item*

14. Find the slope of the line that contains the given pair of points.
    (a, b) and (c, d)

    [A] $\dfrac{b-d}{c-a}$ [B] $\dfrac{a-c}{d-b}$ [C] $\dfrac{d-b}{c-a}$ [D] $\dfrac{a-c}{b-d}$

[5.2.2.15] *Dynamic Item*

15. Find the slope of the line that contains the given pair of points.
    $(-8, -5)$ and $(-2, -5)$

[5.2.2.16] *Dynamic Item*

16. Find the slope of the line that contains the given pair of points.
    $\left(8\dfrac{3}{4}, -9\dfrac{3}{4}\right)$ and $\left(-6\dfrac{1}{4}, -4\dfrac{1}{4}\right)$

Lesson 3: Rate of Change and Direct Variation

Objective 1: Find the rate of change from a graph.

[5.3.1.17] *Dynamic Item*

17. The graph shows the number of dollars that can be bought for a number of pounds. Which is the exchange rate for the number of dollars per pound?

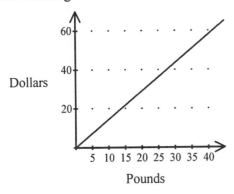

[A] 1.45   [B] 1.07   [C] 0.69   [D] 0.52

[5.3.1.18] *Dynamic Item*

18. The graph for a stable that charges a $10 flat fee plus an hourly rate is shown below. Which is the hourly rate charged?

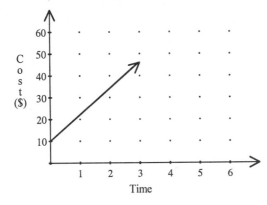

[A] $12 per hour   [B] $6 per hour   [C] $7 per hour   [D] $17 per hour

Lesson 3: Rate of Change and Direct Variation

[5.3.1.19] *Dynamic Item*

19. The figure below represents the distance traveled by a car in 6 hours. Find the speed of the car.

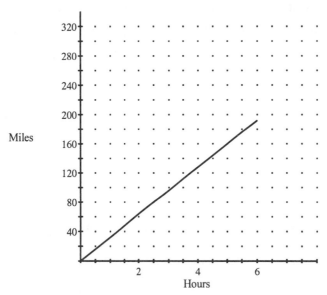

[5.3.1.20] *Dynamic Item*

20. The graph below represents a bicycle rider going uphill, downhill and riding on level pavement at different times. At which times was she doing each of these?

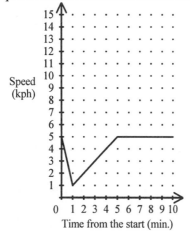

Lesson 3: Rate of Change and Direct Variation

Objective 2: Solve and graph direct-variation equations.

[5.3.2.21] *Dynamic Item*

21. The number of gears G a machine can make varies directly as the time T of operation. If it can make 1152 gears in 6 hours, how many gears can it make in 8 hours?

   [A] 864   [B] 648   [C] 1536   [D] 1920

[5.3.2.22] *Dynamic Item*

22. If $x = 56$ when $y = 140$ and x varies directly as y, then find x when $y = 150$.

   [A] 60   [B] 70   [C] 65   [D] 50

[5.3.2.23] *Dynamic Item*

23. The amount a spring will stretch, S, varies directly as the force (or weight) F attached to the spring. If a spring stretches 3.2 inches when 40 pounds are attached, write a direct variation equation for S in terms of F and find the amount the spring stretches when 10 pounds are attached?

[5.3.2.24] *Dynamic Item*

24. The data below show direct variation. Find the constant of variation and write an equation of direct variation.

Time (hours)	2	4	6	8
Distance (miles)	114	228	342	456

Lesson 4: The Slope-Intercept Form

Objective 1: Define and explain the components of the slope-intercept form of a linear equation.

[5.4.1.25] *Dynamic Item*

25. Which is the equation of the line with slope $\dfrac{3}{2}$ which crosses the y-axis at 2?

[A] $y = \dfrac{3}{2}x - 2$ [B] $y = -\dfrac{3}{2}x - 2$ [C] $x = \dfrac{3}{2}y + 2$ [D] $y = \dfrac{3}{2}x + 2$

[5.4.1.26] *Dynamic Item*

26. Which is the equation of the line graphed below?

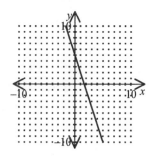

[A] $y = 5x - 3$ [B] $y = -3y + 5$ [C] $y = 3x - 5$ [D] $y = -3x + 5$

[5.4.1.27] *Dynamic Item*

27. Find the slope and the *y*-intercept for the graph of the line with the equation $y = -\dfrac{5}{3}x - 5.$

[5.4.1.28] *Dynamic Item*

28. Without graphing, determine the slope and the *y*-intercept: $y = -3x - 3$

Lesson 4: The Slope-Intercept Form

Objective 2: Use the slope-intercept form of a linear equation.

[5.4.2.29] *Dynamic Item*

29. Write an equation in slope-intercept form for the line graphed.

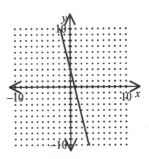

[A] $x = -4y + 3$ [B] $y = 4x - 3$ [C] $y = -4x + 3$ [D] $y = 3x - 4$

Lesson 4: The Slope-Intercept Form

[5.4.2.30] *Dynamic Item*

30. Find the *x*-intercept and *y*-intercept of the graph of the equation: $y = -3x - 5$

[A] $-\dfrac{5}{3}, -5$

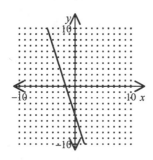

[B] $-3, -5$

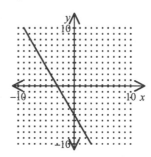

[C] $-5, -3$

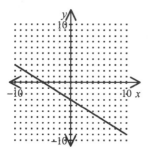

[D] $-5, -\dfrac{5}{3}$

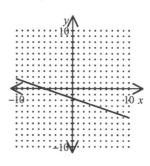

[5.4.2.31] *Dynamic Item*

31. Write an equation in slope-intercept form for the line that contains the given points. $(-8, 2)$ and $(-4, 7)$

[5.4.2.32] *Dynamic Item*

32. A man decides to take out $180 per month from his savings account. He has $25,660 in his account at the beginning. Write a linear equation which models the amount in the savings account in terms of the number of months he withdraws money.

Lesson 5: The Standard and Point-Slope Forms

Objective 1: Define and use the standard form for a linear equation.

[5.5.1.33] *Dynamic Item*

33. Write the equation in standard form: $y = -\dfrac{1}{2}x + 3$

   [A] $x = -\dfrac{1}{2}y + 3$ [B] $-2x = y + 6$ [C] $-2y = x + 6$ [D] $x + 2y = 6$

[5.5.1.34] *Dynamic Item*

34. Find the x- and y-intercepts for the graph of the equation: $-7x + 3y = 9$

   [A] $-1\dfrac{2}{7}, 3$ [B] $-7, 3$ [C] $-\dfrac{7}{9}, \dfrac{1}{3}$ [D] $16, 6$

[5.5.1.35] *Dynamic Item*

35. Write the equation in standard form: $4y = -3x + 28$

[5.5.1.36] *Dynamic Item*

36. Write the equation in standard form: $y + 4 = \dfrac{5}{6}(x + 2)$

Lesson 5: The Standard and Point-Slope Forms

Objective 2: Define and use the point-slope form for a linear equation.

[5.5.2.37] *Dynamic Item*

37. Write an equation in point-slope form for the line that has the given slope and that contains the given point: slope $-\frac{1}{2}$, $(-1,\ -3)$

[A] $y+3=-\frac{1}{2}(x+1)$ [B] $y+1=-\frac{1}{2}(x+3)$

[C] $y-1=-\frac{1}{2}(x-3)$ [D] $y-3=-\frac{1}{2}(x-1)$

[5.5.2.38] *Dynamic Item*

38. The graph of $y+2=\frac{1}{2}(x+8)$ contains which point?

[A] $(8,\ 2)$ [B] $(-2,\ -8)$ [C] $(2,\ 8)$ [D] $(-8,\ -2)$

[5.5.2.39] *Dynamic Item*

39. Write an equation in point-slope form for the line that contains the given points:
(3, –2) and (–5, 1). Use (3, –2) as the point $(x_1,\ y_1)$.

[5.5.2.40] *Dynamic Item*

40. Write the point-slope form of the equation of the line that passes through $(-3,\ 6)$ and has the slope $m=-3$.

Lesson 6: Parallel and Perpendicular Lines

Objective 1: Identify parallel lines and perpendicular lines by comparing their slopes.

[5.6.1.41] *Dynamic Item*

41. Which is the slope of a line that is perpendicular to the graph of $y = -2x$?

[A] $-\dfrac{1}{2}$ [B] -2 [C] $\dfrac{1}{2}$ [D] 2

[5.6.1.42] *Dynamic Item*

42. Which is the slope of a line parallel to the line $4x + 3y = 6$?

[A] $-\dfrac{3}{4}$ [B] $\dfrac{4}{3}$ [C] $\dfrac{3}{4}$ [D] $-\dfrac{4}{3}$

[5.6.1.43] *Dynamic Item*

43. What is the equation of the line perpendicular to the line with zero slope passing through the point $(-3, -9)$?

[5.6.1.44] *Dynamic Item*

44. Find the slope of the line perpendicular to the line $y = 4x - 4$.

Objective 2: Write equations of lines that are parallel and perpendicular to given lines.

[5.6.2.45] *Dynamic Item*

45. Which is the equation in standard form of the line that is perpendicular to $5x + 9y = -4$ and contains $(3, 7)$?

[A] $3x + 7y = 58$ [B] $9x + 5y = 62$ [C] $9x - 5y = -8$ [D] $5x - 9y = -48$

Lesson 6: Parallel and Perpendicular Lines

[5.6.2.46] *Dynamic Item*

46. Which is the equation in slope-intercept form of the line that is parallel to $y = 2x - \dfrac{1}{3}$ and contains $(8,\ 7)$?

    [A] $y = 2x - 9$ [B] $x = 2y - 9$ [C] $y = -\dfrac{1}{2}x - 9$ [D] $x = -\dfrac{1}{2}y - 9$

[5.6.2.47] *Dynamic Item*

47. Write the equation in standard form of the line that is parallel to $-5x - 7y = -3$ and contains $(-7,\ 8)$.

[5.6.2.48] *Dynamic Item*

48. Write the equation in slope-intercept form for the line that contains $(3,\ -1)$ and is perpendicular to the line $-4x - 3y = 3x - 4y$.

Lesson 1: Linear Functions and Graphs

Objective 1: Determine whether a relation is a function.

[5.1.1.1] *Dynamic Item*

[1] [C]

[5.1.1.2] *Dynamic Item*

[2] [C]

[5.1.1.3] *Dynamic Item*

[3] Answers will vary. One possible answer is $(5, 8)$

[5.1.1.4] *Dynamic Item*

[4] No, it is not a function. At least one first coordinate is paired with more than one second coordinate.

Objective 2: Describe the domain and range of a function.

[5.1.2.5] *Dynamic Item*

[5] [A]

[5.1.2.6] *Dynamic Item*

[6] [D]

[5.1.2.7] *Dynamic Item*

[7] $1 \le T \le 4,\ 10 \le H \le 30$

[5.1.2.8] *Dynamic Item*

Number of hours worked	Total Cost
1	$72
2	$104
3	$136
4	$168
5	$200

$C = 32n + 40$

Domain: $\{$positive integers $\leq 100\}$

[8]   Range: $\{x \mid x = 32n + 40;\ n \in$ positive integers $\leq 100\}$

Lesson 2: Defining Slope

Objective 1: Calculate the slope of a line using the rise and run.

[5.2.1.9] *Dynamic Item*

[9] [D]

[5.2.1.10] *Dynamic Item*

[10] [A]

[5.2.1.11] *Dynamic Item*

[11] $-\dfrac{1}{3}$

[5.2.1.12] *Dynamic Item*

[12] undefined

Objective 2: Calculate the slope of a line from the ratio of the differences in *x*- and *y*-coordinates.

[5.2.2.13] *Dynamic Item*

[13] [A]

[5.2.2.14] *Dynamic Item*

[14] [C]

[5.2.2.15] *Dynamic Item*

[15] 0

[5.2.2.16] *Dynamic Item*

[16] $-\dfrac{11}{30}$

Lesson 3: Rate of Change and Direct Variation

Objective 1: Find the rate of change from a graph.

[5.3.1.17] *Dynamic Item*

[17] [A]

[5.3.1.18] *Dynamic Item*

[18] [A]

[5.3.1.19] *Dynamic Item*

[19] The car has traveled 192 miles in 6 hours. Its rate is 32 miles per hour.

[5.3.1.20] *Dynamic Item*

[20] The biker rides uphill for 1 minute, downhill for 4 minutes, then rides on a level street for 5 minutes.

Algebra 1

Objective 2: Solve and graph direct-variation equations.

[5.3.2.21] *Dynamic Item*

[21] [C]

[5.3.2.22] *Dynamic Item*

[22] [A]

[5.3.2.23] *Dynamic Item*

[23] $S = 0.08F$; 0.8 in.

[5.3.2.24] *Dynamic Item*

[24] 57; $d = 57t$

Lesson 4: The Slope-Intercept Form

Objective 1: Define and explain the components of the slope-intercept form of a linear equation.

[5.4.1.25] *Dynamic Item*

[25] [D]

[5.4.1.26] *Dynamic Item*

[26] [D]

[5.4.1.27] *Dynamic Item*

[27] $m = -\dfrac{5}{3}, b = -5$

[5.4.1.28] *Dynamic Item*

[28] The slope is –3 and the y-intercept is –3.

Objective 2: Use the slope-intercept form of a linear equation.

[5.4.2.29] *Dynamic Item*

[29] [C]

[5.4.2.30] *Dynamic Item*

[30] [A]

[5.4.2.31] *Dynamic Item*

[31] $y = \dfrac{5}{4}x + 12$

[5.4.2.32] *Dynamic Item*

[32] $y = 25,660 - 180x$

Lesson 5: The Standard and Point-Slope Forms

Objective 1: Define and use the standard form for a linear equation.

[5.5.1.33] *Dynamic Item*

[33] [D]

[5.5.1.34] *Dynamic Item*

[34] [A]

[5.5.1.35] *Dynamic Item*

[35] $3x + 4y = 28$

[5.5.1.36] *Dynamic Item*

[36] $5x - 6y = 14$

Objective 2: Define and use the point-slope form for a linear equation.

[5.5.2.37] *Dynamic Item*

[37] [A]

[5.5.2.38] *Dynamic Item*

[38] [D]

[5.5.2.39] *Dynamic Item*

[39] $y + 2 = -\dfrac{3}{8}(x - 3)$

[5.5.2.40] *Dynamic Item*

[40] $y - 6 = -3(x + 3)$

Lesson 6: Parallel and Perpendicular Lines

Objective 1: Identify parallel lines and perpendicular lines by comparing their slopes.

[5.6.1.41] *Dynamic Item*

[41] [C]

[5.6.1.42] *Dynamic Item*

[42] [D]

[5.6.1.43] *Dynamic Item*

[43] $x = -3$

[5.6.1.44] *Dynamic Item*

[44] $-\dfrac{1}{4}$

Objective 2: Write equations of lines that are parallel and perpendicular to given lines.

[5.6.2.45] *Dynamic Item*

[45] [C]

[5.6.2.46] *Dynamic Item*

[46] [A]

[5.6.2.47] *Dynamic Item*

[47] $5x + 7y = 21$

[5.6.2.48] *Dynamic Item*

[48] $y = -\dfrac{1}{7}x - \dfrac{4}{7}$

Lesson 1: Solving Inequalities

Objective 1: State and use symbols of inequality.

[6.1.1.1] *Dynamic Item*

1. Which inequality does the graph represent?

    [A] $x > -4$ [B] $x \geq -4$ [C] $x \leq -4$ [D] $x < -4$

[6.1.1.2] *Dynamic Item*

2. Which inequality represents the following situation?
    Julia scored at least 58 points.

    [A] $k > 58$ [B] $k \leq 58$ [C] $k \geq 58$ [D] $k < 58$

[6.1.1.3] *Dynamic Item*

3. Write an inequality to represent the following situation.
    There can be no more than 44 birds in the aviary.

[6.1.1.4] *Dynamic Item*

4. Graph $m < 2$ on a number line.

Objective 2: Solve inequalities that involve addition and subtraction.

[6.1.2.5] *Dynamic Item*

5. Solve the inequality.   [A] $x > 23$ [B] $x > 33$ [C] $x < 23$ [D] $x < 33$
    $x + 5 < 28$

Lesson 1: Solving Inequalities

[6.1.2.6] *Dynamic Item*

6. Solve the inequality.
$$x + \frac{10}{7} \geq -\frac{9}{5}$$

    [A] $x \geq -\frac{35}{113}$ [B] $x \geq \frac{113}{35}$ [C] $x \geq -\frac{113}{35}$ [D] $x \geq -\frac{13}{35}$

[6.1.2.7] *Dynamic Item*

7. Solve the inequality.
$m + 6.6 \leq 55.5$

[6.1.2.8] *Dynamic Item*

8. The maximum weight allowed per car on The Wildcat carnival ride is 260 pounds. Your friend weighs 100 pounds. To be able to ride in a car together how much can you weigh? Write and solve an inequality.

Lesson 2: Multistep Inequalities

Objective 1: State and apply the Multiplication and Division Properties of Inequality.

[6.2.1.9] *Dynamic Item*

9. Solve the inequality.   [A] $t \geq -600$ [B] $t \geq -6$ [C] $t \leq -6$ [D] $t \leq -600$
$10t \geq -60$

[6.2.1.10] *Dynamic Item*

10. Solve the inequality.   [A] $x \leq 1$ [B] $x \geq 90$ [C] $x < 1$ [D] $x > -19$
$$\frac{x}{-9} \leq -10$$

Lesson 2: Multistep Inequalities

[6.2.1.11] *Dynamic Item*

11. Solve the inequality.

    $\dfrac{x}{4} < 11$

[6.2.1.12] *Dynamic Item*

12. Solve the inequality.
    $-5p > 35$

Objective 2: Solve multistep inequalities in one variable.

[6.2.2.13] *Dynamic Item*

13. Solve the inequality.   [A] $x < -8$ [B] $x < -\dfrac{1}{8}$ [C] $x \geq -\dfrac{1}{8}$ [D] $x > -8$

    $-\dfrac{x}{8} - 7 > -6$

[6.2.2.14] *Dynamic Item*

14. Solve the inequality.   [A] $x > 2.5$ [B] $x \geq 2.5$ [C] $x \leq 2.5$ [D] $x < 2.5$

    $5x + 1 \geq 3(x + 2)$

[6.2.2.15] *Dynamic Item*

15. Solve the inequality.
    $12 + 0.5x \geq 0.6(x + 5)$

[6.2.2.16] *Dynamic Item*

16. Solve the inequality.
    $19b - 2 \leq 20b + 5$

Lesson 3: Compound Inequalities

Objective 1: Graph the solution sets of compound inequalities.

[6.3.1.17] *Dynamic Item*

17. Which of the following is the graph of $-4 \le x \le -1$?

[A] 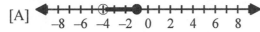   [B]

[C] 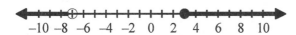   [D]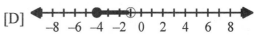

[6.3.1.18] *Dynamic Item*

18. Which inequality does the graph represent?

   [A] $x < -7$ OR $x \ge 3$ [B] $-7 < x \le 3$ [C] $x \le -7$ OR $x > 3$ [D] $-7 \le x < 3$

[6.3.1.19] *Dynamic Item*

19. Graph the compound inequality.
    $x < -7$ OR $x \ge 6$

[6.3.1.20] *Dynamic Item*

20. Graph the compound inequality.
    $-6 \le x < 7$

Objective 2: Solve compound inequalities.

[6.3.2.21] *Dynamic Item*

21. Solve the compound inequality.
    $3x - 3 > 6$ OR $2x + 5 > 19$

   [A] $x < 7$ [B] $x > 3$ [C] all real numbers   [D] no solution

Lesson 3: Compound Inequalities

[6.3.2.22] *Dynamic Item*

22. Solve the compound inequality.
    $-6 \le -2x + 6 \le 10$

    [A] $0 \le x \le 16$ [B] $-2 \le x \le 6$ [C] $6 \le x \le -2$ [D] $16 \le x \le 0$

[6.3.2.23] *Dynamic Item*

23. Zoe makes $9.75 an hour working at Hotdogville. She plans to buy a stereo system for her car, the least expensive of which costs $329.70 and the most expensive of which costs $626.43. Write an inequality describing how long Zoe will have to work to be able to buy a stereo system for her car.

[6.3.2.24] *Dynamic Item*

24. Solve and graph the compound inequality.
    $-6 \le -2x - 4 \le 4$

Lesson 4: Absolute-Value Functions

Objective 1: Explore features of the absolute-value function.

[6.4.1.25] *Dynamic Item*

25. Evaluate.   [A] 2   [B] –2   [C] 34   [D] –34
    $\left| 18 - (-16) \right|$

[6.4.1.26] *Dynamic Item*

26. Evaluate.   [A] –19   [B] 19   [C] 3   [D] –3
    $\left| 11 + (-8) \right|$

[6.4.1.27] *Dynamic Item*

27. Evaluate.
    $\left| f - g \right|$ for $f = 8$, $g = 2$.

Lesson 4: Absolute-Value Functions

[6.4.1.28] *Dynamic Item*

28. Find the absolute value of 94.6.

Objective 2: Explore basic transformations of the absolute-value function.

[6.4.2.29] *Dynamic Item*

29. Which is the graph of $y = |x|$ and its translation to the graph of $y = |x-2|+1$?

[A]

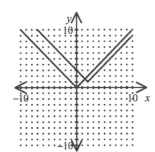

[B]

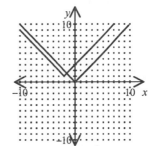

[C]

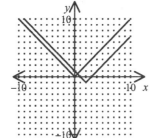

[D]

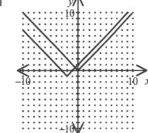

Lesson 4: Absolute-Value Functions

[6.4.2.30] *Dynamic Item*

30. Which is the graph of $y = 5|x| - 5$?

[A]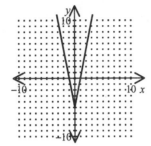

[B]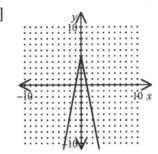

[C]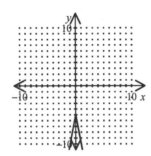

[D]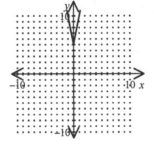

[6.4.2.31] *Dynamic Item*

31. Find the domain and range of $y = -\dfrac{3}{4}|x| + 4$.

[6.4.2.32] *Dynamic Item*

32. Graph the absolute-value functions $y = |x - 2|$ and $y = |x| - 2$ on the same coordinate plane.

Lesson 5: Absolute-Value Equations and Inequalities

Objective 1: Solve absolute-value equations.

[6.5.1.33] *Dynamic Item*

33. Solve the equation if possible. Check your answers.
$$|x + 3| = 5$$

[A] –8   [B] 2, –8   [C] –2   [D] 8, –2

[6.5.1.34] *Dynamic Item*

34. Solve the equation if possible. Check your answers.
$$|5x - 4| = 5$$

[A] $-\dfrac{9}{5}, -\dfrac{1}{5}$ [B] 2, 1   [C] $\dfrac{9}{5}, -\dfrac{1}{5}$ [D] $-\dfrac{13}{5}, 1$

[6.5.1.35] *Dynamic Item*

35. Solve the equation if possible. Check your answers.
$$-25 = |x + 2|$$

[6.5.1.36] *Dynamic Item*

36. Solve the equation if possible. Check your answers.
$$5.4 = |-1.6 + 9x|$$

Lesson 5: Absolute-Value Equations and Inequalities

Objective 2: Solve absolute-value inequalities, and express the solution as a range of values on a number line.

[6.5.2.37] *Dynamic Item*

37. Solve the inequality. Check your answers.

$$|4x-1| \geq 4$$

[A] $x \leq -\dfrac{3}{4}$ OR $x \geq \dfrac{5}{4}$ [B] $-\dfrac{3}{4} \leq x \leq \dfrac{5}{4}$

[C] $x < -\dfrac{3}{4}$ OR $x > \dfrac{5}{4}$ [D] none of these

[6.5.2.38] *Dynamic Item*

38. Solve the inequality. Check your answers.

$$|x-3| \leq 1$$

[A] $x \leq 2$ OR $x \geq 4$ [B] $x \leq 2$ [C] $2 \leq x \leq 4$ [D] $x < 2$ OR $x > 4$

[6.5.2.39] *Dynamic Item*

39. Solve the inequality. Check your answers.

$$|5-0.25x| > 11$$

[6.5.2.40] *Dynamic Item*

40. Solve the inequality. Check your answers.

$$\left|\dfrac{4}{7}x-3\right| > 9$$

Lesson 1: Solving Inequalities

Objective 1: State and use symbols of inequality.

[6.1.1.1] *Dynamic Item*

[1] [A]

[6.1.1.2] *Dynamic Item*

[2] [C]

[6.1.1.3] *Dynamic Item*

[3] $n \le 44$

[6.1.1.4] *Dynamic Item*

[4]

Objective 2: Solve inequalities that involve addition and subtraction.

[6.1.2.5] *Dynamic Item*

[5] [C]

[6.1.2.6] *Dynamic Item*

[6] [C]

[6.1.2.7] *Dynamic Item*

[7] $m \le 48.9$

[6.1.2.8] *Dynamic Item*

[8] $x + 100 \le 260$; at most 160 pounds

Lesson 2: Multistep Inequalities

Objective 1: State and apply the Multiplication and Division Properties of Inequality.

[6.2.1.9] *Dynamic Item*

 [9] [B]

[6.2.1.10] *Dynamic Item*

[10] [B]

[6.2.1.11] *Dynamic Item*

[11] $x < 44$

[6.2.1.12] *Dynamic Item*

[12] $p < -7$

Objective 2: Solve multistep inequalities in one variable.

[6.2.2.13] *Dynamic Item*

[13] [A]

[6.2.2.14] *Dynamic Item*

[14] [B]

[6.2.2.15] *Dynamic Item*

[15] $x \leq 90$

[6.2.2.16] *Dynamic Item*

[16] $b \geq -7$

Lesson 3: Compound Inequalities

Objective 1: Graph the solution sets of compound inequalities.

[6.3.1.17] *Dynamic Item*

[17] [B]

[6.3.1.18] *Dynamic Item*

[18] [A]

[6.3.1.19] *Dynamic Item*

[19]
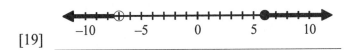

[6.3.1.20] *Dynamic Item*

[20]
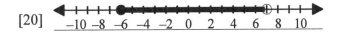

Objective 2: Solve compound inequalities.

[6.3.2.21] *Dynamic Item*

[21] [B]

[6.3.2.22] *Dynamic Item*

[22] [B]

[6.3.2.23] *Dynamic Item*

[23] Answers may vary. One possible answer is $\$329.70 \le \$9.75h \le \$626.43$

[6.3.2.24] *Dynamic Item*

[24]

Lesson 4: Absolute-Value Functions

Objective 1: Explore features of the absolute-value function.

[6.4.1.25] *Dynamic Item*

[25] [C]

[6.4.1.26] *Dynamic Item*

[26] [C]

[6.4.1.27] *Dynamic Item*

[27] 6

[6.4.1.28] *Dynamic Item*

[28] 94.6

Objective 2: Explore basic transformations of the absolute-value function.

[6.4.2.29] *Dynamic Item*

[29] [A]

[6.4.2.30] *Dynamic Item*

[30] [A]

[6.4.2.31] *Dynamic Item*

Domain: all real numbers
[31] Range: $y \le 4$

[6.4.2.32] *Dynamic Item*

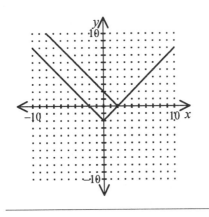

[32]

Lesson 5: Absolute-Value Equations and Inequalities

Objective 1: Solve absolute-value equations.

[6.5.1.33] *Dynamic Item*

[33] [B]

[6.5.1.34] *Dynamic Item*

[34] [C]

[6.5.1.35] *Dynamic Item*

[35] No Solution

[6.5.1.36] *Dynamic Item*

[36] 0.777778, −0.422222

Objective 2: Solve absolute-value inequalities, and express the solution as a range of values on a number line.

[6.5.2.37] *Dynamic Item*

[37] [A]

[6.5.2.38] *Dynamic Item*

[38] [C]

[6.5.2.39] *Dynamic Item*

[39] $x < -24$ OR $x > 64$

[6.5.2.40] *Dynamic Item*

[40] $x < -\dfrac{21}{2}$ OR $x > 21$

Lesson 1: Graphing Systems of Equations

Objective 1: Graph systems of equations.

[7.1.1.1] *Dynamic Item*

1. Which is the graph of the system?
$$\begin{cases} x+y=-1 \\ 3x-y=5 \end{cases}$$

[A]
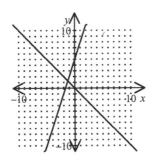

[B]
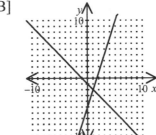

[C]
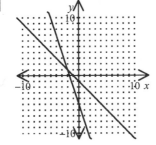

[D]
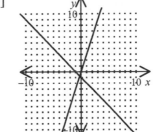

Lesson 1: Graphing Systems of Equations

[7.1.1.2] *Dynamic Item*

2. Which is the graph of the system?
$$\begin{cases} y = -2 - x \\ y = 3x - 6 \end{cases}$$

[A]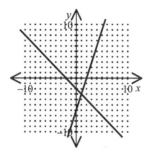

[B]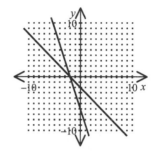

[C]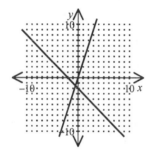

[D]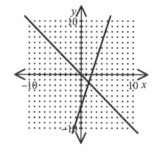

[7.1.1.3] *Dynamic Item*

3. Graph the system of equations.
$$\begin{cases} x + y = -1 \\ y = 2x - 7 \end{cases}$$

[7.1.1.4] *Dynamic Item*

4. Graph the system of equations.
$$\begin{cases} 3x = 2y - 3 \\ 3y = 2x + 7 \end{cases}$$

Lesson 1: Graphing Systems of Equations

Objective 2: Solve a system of equations by inspecting a graph.

[7.1.2.5] *Dynamic Item*

5. Which of the following ordered pairs is a solution of the system?
$$\begin{cases} -9x - 3y = -5 \\ -6x - 9y = 4 \end{cases}$$

[A] $(-1, \ 0.9)$ [B] $(0.9, \ 1)$

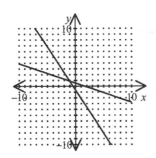   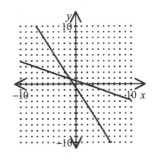

[C] $(0.9, \ -1)$ [D] $(-0.9, \ -1)$

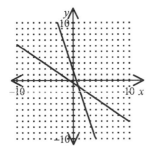   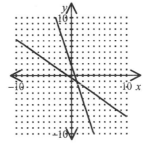

[7.1.2.6] *Dynamic Item*

6. Which of the following ordered pairs is a solution of the system?
$$\begin{cases} 2x + 3y = -45 \\ -6x + 5y = 9 \end{cases}$$

[A] (−9, −9)   [B] (−7, −10)   [C] (−13, −11)   [D] (−10, −7)

Lesson 1: Graphing Systems of Equations

[7.1.2.7] *Dynamic Item*

7. Solve by graphing. Round approximate solutions to the nearest tenth.
$$\begin{cases} y = 3x - 11 \\ y = -4x + 10 \end{cases}$$

[7.1.2.8] *Dynamic Item*

8. TV Repair by Tomas charges $73 for parts and $28 per hour of labor for a repair job. Tolliver's TV Shop charges a flat fee of $145 for the same job.
   a. Write a system of equations to represent the situation.
   b. Graph the system of equations.
   c. Which shop is cheaper if the job takes 2 hours? 3 hours? 4 hours?

Lesson 2: The Substitution Method

Objective 1: Find an exact solution to a system of linear equations by using the substitution method.

[7.2.1.9] *Dynamic Item*

9. Solve by using substitution.
$$\begin{cases} x + 2y = 1 \\ x = -9 + 3y \end{cases}$$

[A] $(3, -2)$ [B] $(-2, -15)$ [C] $(-3, 2)$ [D] $\left(2, -\dfrac{1}{2}\right)$

[7.2.1.10] *Dynamic Item*

10. Solve by using substitution.
$$\begin{cases} y = 2x + 2 \\ y = 3x \end{cases}$$

[A] $(3, 9)$ [B] $(1, 4)$ [C] $(-2, -4)$ [D] $(2, 6)$

Algebra 1

Lesson 2: The Substitution Method

[7.2.1.11] *Dynamic Item*

11. Solve by using substitution.

$$\begin{cases} 2x+4y=2 \\ x-4y=-11 \end{cases}$$

[7.2.1.12] *Dynamic Item*

12. One of the acute angles in a right triangle measures 6° less than 11 times the other acute angle. What is the measure of each acute angle? The sum of the two acute angles in a right triangle is 90°. Write a system of two equations in two unknowns and solve.

Lesson 3: The Elimination Method

Objective 1: Use the elimination method to solve a system of equations.

[7.3.1.13] *Dynamic Item*

13. Solve the system of equations by elimination.

$$\begin{cases} 5x-2y=-1 \\ 4x-5y=3 \end{cases}$$

[A] $\left(-\dfrac{11}{17}, -\dfrac{19}{17}\right)$ [B] $\left(-\dfrac{19}{17}, -\dfrac{11}{17}\right)$ [C] $\left(\dfrac{1}{33}, -\dfrac{1}{3}\right)$ [D] $\left(-\dfrac{1}{3}, \dfrac{1}{33}\right)$

[7.3.1.14] *Dynamic Item*

14. Solve the system of equations by elimination.

$$\begin{cases} 2x-3y=-7 \\ x+3y=-8 \end{cases}$$

[A] $\left(-1, \dfrac{5}{3}\right)$ [B] $(-17, -1)$ [C] $(-5, -1)$ [D] $\left(0, \dfrac{7}{3}\right)$

Lesson 3: The Elimination Method

[7.3.1.15] *Dynamic Item*

15. Solve the system of equations by elimination.
$$\begin{cases} 9x - 5y = 88 \\ 7x - 4y = 69 \end{cases}$$

[7.3.1.16] *Dynamic Item*

16. The Modern Grocery has cashews that sell for $4.25 a pound and peanuts that sell for $2.00 a pound. Write and solve a system of equations in two variables to find how much of each that Albert, the grocer, should mix to get 90 pounds of mixture that he can sell for $3.00 per pound.

Objective 2: Choose an appropriate method to solve a system of equations.

[7.3.2.17] *Dynamic Item*

17. An ice skating arena charges an admission fee for each child plus a rental fee for each pair of ice skates. Nelson paid the admission fees for his three nephews and rented two pairs of ice skates. He was charged $22.50. Bernice paid the admission fees for her five grandchildren and rented three pairs of ice skates. She was charged $36.50. What is the admission fee? What is the rental fee for a pair of skates?

[A] admission fee: $5.75
   skate rental fee: $3.50

[B] admission fee: $6.25
   skate rental fee: $4.00

[C] admission fee: $5.25
   skate rental fee: $2.50

[D] admission fee: $5.50
   skate rental fee: $3.00

[7.3.2.18] *Dynamic Item*

18. Solve by any method.
$$\begin{cases} \dfrac{x}{4} - \dfrac{y}{3} = -\dfrac{5}{12} \\ 9x + 2y = -29 \end{cases}$$

[A] $\left(-2, -\dfrac{1}{4}\right)$
[B] $\left(\dfrac{1}{2}, -1\right)$
[C] $\left(-1, \dfrac{1}{2}\right)$
[D] $(-3, -1)$

Lesson 3: The Elimination Method

[7.3.2.19] *Dynamic Item*

19. Solve by any method.
$$\begin{cases} 3x + 2y = -20 \\ y = 3x + 8 \end{cases}$$

[7.3.2.20] *Dynamic Item*

20. A rental car agency charges $15 per day plus 14 cents per mile to rent a certain car. Another agency charges $22 per day plus 9 cents per mile to rent the same car. How many miles will have to be driven in order for the cost of a car from the first agency to equal the cost of a car from the second agency? (Round your answer to the nearest hundredth of a mile.) Express the problem as a system of linear equations and solve using the method of your choice.

Lesson 4: Consistent and Inconsistent Systems

Objective 1: Identify consistent and inconsistent systems of equations.

[7.4.1.21] *Dynamic Item*

21. Identify the correct graph and classification of the following system.
$$\begin{cases} y - x = 1 \\ 2y - 2x = 4 \end{cases}$$

[A]

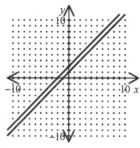

consistent

[B]

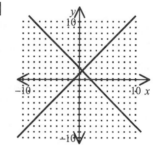

consistent

[C]

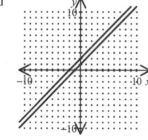

inconsistent

[D]

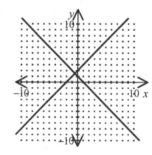

inconsistent

[7.4.1.22] *Dynamic Item*

22. Without graphing, classify this system and determine the number of solutions.
$$\begin{cases} -4x + 4y = -16 \\ -12x + 12y = -96 \end{cases}$$

[A] inconsistent, no solution

[B] inconsistent, infinitely many solutions

[C] consistent, one solution

[D] consistent, infinitely many solutions

Lesson 4: Consistent and Inconsistent Systems

[7.4.1.23] *Dynamic Item*

23. Identify the system as consistent or inconsistent and find the number of solutions.

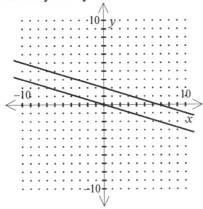

[7.4.1.24] *Dynamic Item*

24. Identify the system of linear equations as consistent or inconsistent.

$$\begin{cases} 3x - y = -3 \\ 9x - 6y = -9 \end{cases}$$

Objective 2: Identify dependent and independent systems of equations.

[7.4.2.25] *Dynamic Item*

25. Solve the system algebraically. Find the number of solutions for the system.

$$\begin{cases} 5x - y = -5 \\ -10x + 2y = 10 \end{cases}$$

[A] infinite number of solutions

[B] one solution

[C] no solutions

[D] none of these

Lesson 4: Consistent and Inconsistent Systems

[7.4.2.26] *Dynamic Item*

26. Which best describes the system?
$$\begin{cases} -3x + 2y = -6 \\ -6x + 4y = -24 \end{cases}$$

    [A] consistent, independent   [B] inconsistent

    [C] consistent, dependent   [D] none of these

[7.4.2.27] *Dynamic Item*

27. Solve the system algebraically. Identify the system as consistent and independent, consistent and dependent or inconsistent.
$$\begin{cases} 6x + 6y = -4 \\ y = -x \end{cases}$$

[7.4.2.28] *Dynamic Item*

28. Solve the system algebraically. Identify the system as consistent and dependent, consistent and independent or inconsistent. Give the number of solutions.
$$\begin{cases} 2x + 2y = 4 \\ -6x - 12y = -12 \end{cases}$$

Lesson 5: Systems of Inequalities

Objective 1: Graph the solution to a linear inequality.

[7.5.1.29] *Dynamic Item*

29. Which is the graph of the inequality?
    $y < -2x + 2$

[A]

[B]

[C]

[D]

Lesson 5: Systems of Inequalities

[7.5.1.30] *Dynamic Item*

30. Which is the graph of the inequality?
$4x - 7y > -28$

[A]

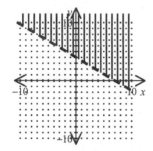

[B]

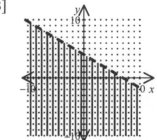

[C]

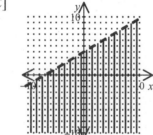

[D]

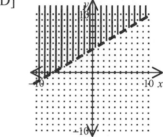

[7.5.1.31] *Dynamic Item*

31. Graph the inequality: $2x + y \geq 2$

[7.5.1.32] *Dynamic Item*

32. An electronics store makes a profit of $145 for every standard CD player sold and $87 for every portable CD player sold. The manager's target is to make at least $435 a day on sales from standard and portable CD players.
a. Write an inequality that represents the numbers of both kinds of CD players that can be sold to reach or beat the sales target.
b. Graph the inequality.

Lesson 5: Systems of Inequalities

Objective 2: Graph the solution to a system of linear inequalities.

[7.5.2.33] *Dynamic Item*

33. Which graph shows the solution to the system of inequalities?
$$\begin{cases} y \le x + 2 \\ x + y \le 5 \end{cases}$$

[A]

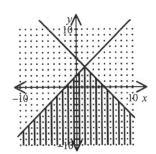

[B]

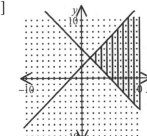

[C]

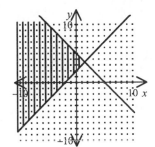

[D]

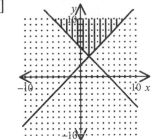

Lesson 5: Systems of Inequalities

[7.5.2.34] *Dynamic Item*

34. Which graph shows the solution to the system of inequalities?
$$\begin{cases} y \le -x - 7 \\ y \ge 2x - 3 \end{cases}$$

[A]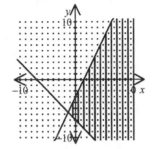

[B]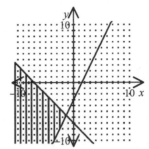

[C]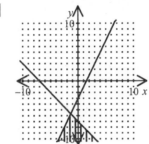

[D]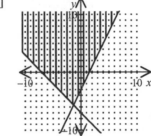

[7.5.2.35] *Dynamic Item*

35. Solve by graphing.
$$\begin{cases} y \ge -\dfrac{1}{2}x + 7 \\ y \le \dfrac{3}{4}x + 2 \end{cases}$$

Lesson 5: Systems of Inequalities

[7.5.2.36] *Dynamic Item*

36. Solve by graphing.

$$\begin{cases} 4x + 3y < 15 \\ -4x - 3y < 15 \end{cases}$$

Lesson 6: Classic Puzzles in Two Variables

Objective 1: Solve traditional math puzzles in two variables.

[7.6.1.37] *Dynamic Item*

37. The sum of the digits of a 2-digit number is 9. If the digits are reversed, the new number is 27 less than the original number. Find the original number.

   [A] 63   [B] 54   [C] 72   [D] 45

[7.6.1.38] *Dynamic Item*

38. Mr. Huang operates a soybean farm outside of Grinnell, Iowa. To keep costs down, he buys many products in bulk and transfers them to smaller containers for use on the farm. Often the bulk products are not the correct concentration and need to be custom mixed before Mr. Huang can use them. One day he wants to apply fertilizer to a large field. A solution of 73% fertilizer is to be mixed with a solution of 57% fertilizer to form 32 liters of a 58% solution. How much of the 73% solution must he use?

   [A] 2 L   [B] 25 L   [C] 3 L   [D] 31 L

[7.6.1.39] *Dynamic Item*

39. A jar filled with only nickels and quarters contains a total of 57 coins. The value of all the coins in the jar is $8.85. How many quarters are in the jar?

[7.6.1.40] *Dynamic Item*

40. Crystal is a bush pilot in Alaska. On a recent trip, she flew 600 miles with a tail wind in four hours. On the return trip, it took five hours to fly the 600 miles against the wind. Find the speed of the plane with no wind.

Lesson 1: Graphing Systems of Equations

Objective 1: Graph systems of equations.

[7.1.1.1] *Dynamic Item*

[1]   [B]

[7.1.1.2] *Dynamic Item*

[2]   [A]

[7.1.1.3] *Dynamic Item*

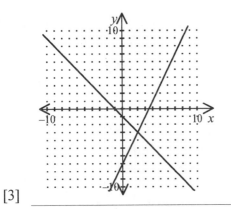

[3]   _____

[7.1.1.4] *Dynamic Item*

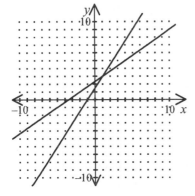

[4]   (1, 3)

Objective 2: Solve a system of equations by inspecting a graph.

[7.1.2.5] *Dynamic Item*

[5]   [C]

[7.1.2.6] *Dynamic Item*

[6]   [A]

[7.1.2.7] *Dynamic Item*

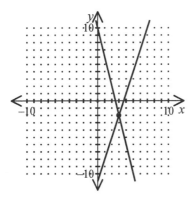

[7]   (3, –2)

[7.1.2.8] *Dynamic Item*

$$\begin{cases} y = 28x + 73 \\ y = 145 \end{cases}$$

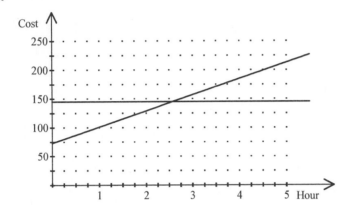

TV Repair by Tomas is cheaper for 2 hours of work.
Tolliver's TV Shop is cheaper for 3 hours of work.

[8]   Tolliver's TV Shop is cheaper for 4 hours of work.

Lesson 2: The Substitution Method

Objective 1: Find an exact solution to a system of linear equations by using the substitution method.

[7.2.1.9] *Dynamic Item*

[9]   [C]

[7.2.1.10] *Dynamic Item*

[10]   [D]

[7.2.1.11] *Dynamic Item*

[11] $(-3, 2)$

[7.2.1.12] *Dynamic Item*

$$\begin{cases} x + y = 90 \\ y = 11x - 6 \end{cases}$$

[12] $x = 8, \; y = 82$

Lesson 3: The Elimination Method

Objective 1: Use the elimination method to solve a system of equations.

[7.3.1.13] *Dynamic Item*

[13] [A]

[7.3.1.14] *Dynamic Item*

[14] [C]

[7.3.1.15] *Dynamic Item*

[15] $(7, \; -5)$

[7.3.1.16] *Dynamic Item*

If c represents the number of pounds of cashews and p represents the number of pounds of peanuts, $\begin{cases} c + p = 90 \\ 4.25\,c + 2.00\,p = 3.00(90). \end{cases}$

$c = 40$ pounds of cashews

[16] $p = 50$ pounds of peanuts

Objective 2: Choose an appropriate method to solve a system of equations.

[7.3.2.17] *Dynamic Item*

[17] [D]

[7.3.2.18] *Dynamic Item*

[18]   [D]

[7.3.2.19] *Dynamic Item*

[19]   (–4, –4)

[7.3.2.20] *Dynamic Item*

$$\begin{cases} c = 15 + 0.14m \\ c = 22 + 0.09m \end{cases}$$

[20]   140 miles

Lesson 4: Consistent and Inconsistent Systems

Objective 1: Identify consistent and inconsistent systems of equations.

[7.4.1.21] *Dynamic Item*

[21]   [C]

[7.4.1.22] *Dynamic Item*

[22]   [A]

[7.4.1.23] *Dynamic Item*

[23]   inconsistent, no solution

[7.4.1.24] *Dynamic Item*

[24]   consistent

Objective 2: Identify dependent and independent systems of equations.

*[7.4.2.25] *Dynamic Item**

[25] [A]

*[7.4.2.26] *Dynamic Item**

[26] [B]

*[7.4.2.27] *Dynamic Item**

[27] inconsistent

*[7.4.2.28] *Dynamic Item**

[28] consistent and independent; one solution

Lesson 5: Systems of Inequalities

Objective 1: Graph the solution to a linear inequality.

*[7.5.1.29] *Dynamic Item**

[29] [A]

*[7.5.1.30] *Dynamic Item**

[30] [C]

[7.5.1.31] *Dynamic Item*

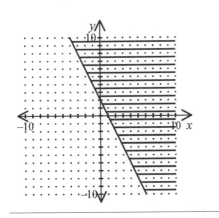

[31] _____

[7.5.1.32] *Dynamic Item*

$$145s + 87p \geq 435$$

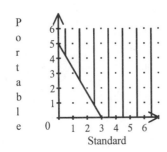

[32] _____

Objective 2: Graph the solution to a system of linear inequalities.

[7.5.2.33] *Dynamic Item*

[33] [A] _____

[7.5.2.34] *Dynamic Item*

[34] [B] _____

[7.5.2.35] *Dynamic Item*

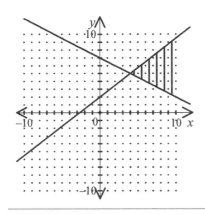

[35] _____

[7.5.2.36] *Dynamic Item*

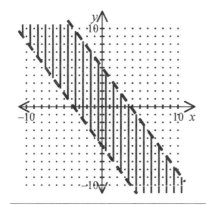

[36] _____

Lesson 6: Classic Puzzles in Two Variables

Objective 1: Solve traditional math puzzles in two variables.

[7.6.1.37] *Dynamic Item*

[37] [A]

[7.6.1.38] *Dynamic Item*

[38] [A]

[7.6.1.39] *Dynamic Item*

[39] 30

[7.6.1.40] *Dynamic Item*

[40] 135 miles per hour

Lesson 1: Laws of Exponents: Multiplying Monomials

Objective 1: Define exponents and powers.

[8.1.1.1] *Dynamic Item*

1. Write the product using exponents: $d \cdot d \cdot d \cdot d \cdot d \cdot d$

   [A] $6d$ [B] d^6 [C] 6^d [D] none of these

[8.1.1.2] *Dynamic Item*

2. Which is the value of 3^6?   [A] 36   [B] 18   [C] 729   [D] 2187

[8.1.1.3] *Dynamic Item*

3. What is the value of 10^3?

[8.1.1.4] *Dynamic Item*

4. A culture of bacteria doubles in size every half-hour. If the colony contained 2400 bacteria at noon, how many bacteria will the culture contain at 4:00 P.M.?

Objective 2: Find products of powers.

[8.1.2.5] *Dynamic Item*

5. Simplify: [A] $2u^4$ [B] u^8 [C] $2u^8$ [D] u^{12}
   $u^2 \cdot u^6$

[8.1.2.6] *Dynamic Item*

6. Simplify: [A] 3^9 [B] 3^{18} [C] 3^3 [D] 9^9
   $3^3 \cdot 3^6$

[8.1.2.7] *Dynamic Item*

7. Simplify:
   $b^6 \cdot b$

Lesson 1: Laws of Exponents: Multiplying Monomials

[8.1.2.8] *Dynamic Item*

8. Simplify the product. Leave the product in exponent form.

$7^4 \cdot 7^{11}$

Objective 3: Simplify products of monomials.

[8.1.3.9] *Dynamic Item*

9. Simplify:

$\left(3n^4\right)\left(-4n^4\right)\left(4n^7\right)$

[A] $-48n^{112}$　[B] $-48n^{15}$　[C] $3n^{15}$　[D] $3n^{112}$

[8.1.3.10] *Dynamic Item*

10. Simplify:

$\left(-2v^4w^3\right)\left(8vw^4\right)$

[A] $16v^4w^4$　[B] $-16v^4w^{12}$　[C] $16v^5w^7$　[D] $-16v^5w^7$

[8.1.3.11] *Dynamic Item*

11. Simplify:

$\left(8x^3y^2\right)\left(4x^4y^2\right)$

[8.1.3.12] *Dynamic Item*

12. A trapezoid has a height of $8xy$ centimeters. Its shorter base is $14y$ centimeters, and its longer base is $22y$ centimeters. Use the formula $A = \frac{1}{2}(b_1 + b_2)h$, where b_1 and b_2 are the bases and h is the height to find the area of the trapezoid.

Lesson 2: Laws of Exponents: Powers and Products

Objective 1: Find the power of a power.

[8.2.1.13] *Dynamic Item*

13. Simplify: [A] $-c^{2/3}$ [B] $-c^6$ [C] $-c^8$ [D] c^5
    $\left(-c^2\right)^3$

[8.2.1.14] *Dynamic Item*

14. Which is the value of $\left(10^2\right)^4$?

    [A] 1,000,000   [B] 10,000   [C] 100,000,000   [D] 160,000

[8.2.1.15] *Dynamic Item*

15. Find the value of the expression.

    $\left(2^4\right)^3$

[8.2.1.16] *Dynamic Item*

16. Simplify:

    $\left(c^3\right)^y$

Objective 2: Find the power of a product.

[8.2.2.17] *Dynamic Item*

17. Simplify:

    $\left(x^2 y^2\right)^3 \left(-3x^4 y^2\right)^3$

    [A] $-26x^{12}y^{10}$ [B] $-26x^{18}y^{12}$ [C] $-27x^{18}y^{12}$ [D] $-27x^{12}y^{10}$

Lesson 2: Laws of Exponents: Powers and Products

[8.2.2.18] *Dynamic Item*

18. Simplify:　　[A] $64b^7$　　　[B] $4096b^{12}$　　　[C] $64b^{12}$　　　[D] $4096b^7$
$8\left(2b^4\right)^3$

[8.2.2.19] *Dynamic Item*

19. Simplify:
$\left(4w^5x^6y\right)^2$

[8.2.2.20] *Dynamic Item*

20. Evaluate $(ka)^e$, for $k = 4$, $a = 10$, and $e = 3$.

Lesson 3: Laws of Exponents: Dividing Monomials

Objective 1: Simplify quotients of powers.

[8.3.1.21] *Dynamic Item*

21. Use the Quotient-of-Powers Property to simplify the quotient.
$$-\frac{e^2 f^4 g^5}{efg}$$

　[A] $-e^3 f^5 g^6$　　　　[B] $\dfrac{1}{ef^3 g^4}$　　　　[C] $-ef^3 g^4$　　　　[D] $ef^3 g^4$

[8.3.1.22] *Dynamic Item*

22. Use the Quotient-of-Powers Property to simplify the quotient.
$$\frac{24x^4 y^5}{-6x^2 y}$$

　[A] $4x^2 y^4$　　　　[B] $-4x^2 y^4$　　　　[C] $-2x^6 y^6$　　　　[D] $2x^6 y^6$

Lesson 3: Laws of Exponents: Dividing Monomials

[8.3.1.23] *Dynamic Item*

23. Use the Quotient-of-Powers Property to simplify the quotient.

$$\frac{1.2d^{16}e^{17}}{4(de)^{12}}$$

[8.3.1.24] *Dynamic Item*

24. Use the Quotient-of-Powers Property to simplify the quotient. Then find the value of the result.

$$\frac{7^{10}}{7^{6}}$$

Objective 2: Simplify powers of fractions.

[8.3.2.25] *Dynamic Item*

25. Simplify the expression. Assume that the conditions of the Quotient-of-Powers Property are met.

$$\left(\frac{4a^{6}b^{6}}{5a^{5}b^{2}}\right)^{3}$$

[A] $\dfrac{4a^{4}b^{7}}{5}$ [B] $\dfrac{4a^{3}b^{12}}{5}$ [C] $\dfrac{64a^{4}b^{7}}{125}$ [D] $\dfrac{64a^{3}b^{12}}{125}$

[8.3.2.26] *Dynamic Item*

26. Simplify the expression. Assume that the conditions of the Quotient-of-Powers Property are met.

$$\left(\frac{q^{7}}{r^{6}}\right)^{5}$$

[A] $\dfrac{q^{35}}{r^{6}}$ [B] $\dfrac{q^{12}}{r^{6}}$ [C] $\dfrac{q^{12}}{r^{11}}$ [D] $\dfrac{q^{35}}{r^{30}}$

Lesson 3: Laws of Exponents: Dividing Monomials

[8.3.2.27] *Dynamic Item*

27. Simplify the expression. Assume that the conditions of the Quotient-of-Powers Property are met.

$$\left(\frac{1}{5}\right)^3$$

[8.3.2.28] *Dynamic Item*

28. Simplify the expression. Assume that the conditions of the Quotient-of-Powers Property are met.

$$\left(\frac{4a^2b^5}{c}\right)^c$$

Lesson 4: Negative and Zero Exponents

Objective 1: Understand the concepts of negative and zero exponents.

[8.4.1.29] *Dynamic Item*

29. Evaluate the expression.   [A] 729   [B] 0   [C] −18   [D] $\dfrac{1}{729}$

$3^{-6} \cdot 3^0$

[8.4.1.30] *Dynamic Item*

30. Evaluate the expression.   [A] $\dfrac{3}{7}$ [B] $\dfrac{4}{7}$ [C] $\dfrac{1}{7}$ [D] $\dfrac{2}{7}$

7^{-1}

[8.4.1.31] *Dynamic Item*

31. Evaluate the expression.

$$\frac{10^0}{10^4}$$

Lesson 4: Negative and Zero Exponents

[8.4.1.32] *Dynamic Item*

32. Simplify and write the expression with positive exponents only: $4x^{-1}y^0$

Objective 2: Simplify expressions containing negative and zero exponents.

[8.4.2.33] *Dynamic Item*

33. Write the following without negative or zero exponents.
$$x^0 x^{-6}$$

    [A] x^0 [B] $\dfrac{1}{x^5}$ [C] x^6 [D] $\dfrac{1}{x^6}$

[8.4.2.34] *Dynamic Item*

34. Write the following without negative or zero exponents.
$$\dfrac{x^{-2}}{x^{-9}}$$

    [A] $\dfrac{1}{x^7}$ [B] x^{11} [C] $\dfrac{1}{x^{11}}$ [D] x^7

[8.4.2.35] *Dynamic Item*

35. Write the following without negative or zero exponents.
$$\dfrac{9a^{-3}b^3}{81a^{-4}b^4}$$

[8.4.2.36] *Dynamic Item*

36. Write the following without negative or zero exponents.
$$\dfrac{18a^3b^2c^{-8}}{3a^0b^{-5}c^3}$$

Lesson 5: Scientific Notation

Objective 1: Recognize the need for special notation in scientific calculations.

[8.5.1.37] *Dynamic Item*

37. A virus takes up a volume of approximately 0.000000000000052 cubic centimeters. What is that value expressed in scientific notation?

[A] 5.2×10^{-14} [B] 5.2×10^{14} [C] 5.2×10^{-15} [D] 5.2×10^{-13}

[8.5.1.38] *Dynamic Item*

38. Write the number in scientific notation.
0.000295

[A] 2.95×10^{5} [B] 295×10^{-4} [C] 2.95×10^{-2} [D] 2.95×10^{-4}

[8.5.1.39] *Dynamic Item*

39. Write the number in scientific notation.
In 1995, Indonesia had a population of about 206,400,000 people.

[8.5.1.40] *Dynamic Item*

40. Write the number in scientific notation.
7,300

Objective 2: Perform computations involving scientific notation.

[8.5.2.41] *Dynamic Item*

41. Astronomers measure large distances in light-years. One light-year is the distance that light can travel in one year, or approximately 5,880,000,000,000 miles. If a star is 8.3 light-years from Earth, which expression in scientific notation correctly represents how far the star is from Earth?

[A] 5.90×10^{12} miles   [B] 48.8×10^{12} miles

[C] 4.88×10^{13} miles   [D] 4.80×10^{13} miles

Lesson 5: Scientific Notation

[8.5.2.42] *Dynamic Item*

42. Perform the following computation: $\dfrac{16\times10^{11}}{4\times10^{2}}$. Which is the answer in scientific notation?

   [A] 4×10^{9} [B] 4×10^{13} [C] 12×10^{13} [D] 6.4×10^{10}

[8.5.2.43] *Dynamic Item*

43. Radio signals travel at a rate of 3.00×10^{8} meters per second. How many seconds will it take for a radio signal to travel from a satellite to the surface of Earth if the satellite is orbiting at a height of 1.44×10^{8} meters?

[8.5.2.44] *Dynamic Item*

44. Perform the following computation: $(7\times10^{4})(9\times10^{9})$. What is the answer in scientific notation?

Lesson 6: Exponential Functions

Objective 1: Understand exponential functions and how they are used.

[8.6.1.45] *Dynamic Item*

45. The inflation rate of the U.S. dollar is 3.3 percent. This means that every year prices increase by 3.3 percent. If a sandwich cost $4.95 eight years ago, what does it cost now? Use the formula $P = A(1+r)^{t}$, where P is the amount an item costs today, A is the amount the item originally cost, r is the interest rate as a decimal, and t is the time in years.

   [A] $3.78   [B] $6.42   [C] $5.11   [D] $38.29

[8.6.1.46] *Dynamic Item*

46. If $1850 is invested in an account which earns 7% interest compounded annually, what will be the balance of the account at the end of 9 years? Use the formula $P = A(1+r)^{t}$, where P is the account balance, A is the amount originally invested, r is the interest rate as a decimal, and t is the time invested in years.

   [A] $3016   [B] $3401   [C] $219,388   [D] $1852

Lesson 6: Exponential Functions

[8.6.1.47] *Dynamic Item*

47. If $1890 is invested in an account which earns 4% interest compounded annually, what will be the balance of the account at the end of 11 years? Use the formula $P = A(1+r)^t$, where P is the account balance, A is the amount originally invested, r is the interest rate as a decimal, and t is the time invested in years. Round your answer to the nearest dollar.

[8.6.1.48] *Dynamic Item*

48. A population of 290 deer return to a forest immediately after a fire. The population increases at an annual rate of 15%. Use the formula $P = A(1+r)^t$, where P is the new population, A is the original population, r is the percent written as a decimal and t is the time in years to find the population 5 years after the fire.

Lesson 6: Exponential Functions

Objective 2: Recognize differences between graphs of exponential functions with different bases.

[8.6.2.49] *Dynamic Item*

49. Which is the graph of the function?

$$y = \left(\frac{1}{10}\right)^x$$

[A]

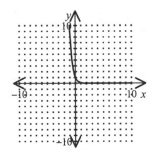

[B]

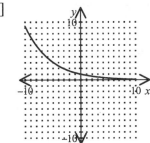

[C]

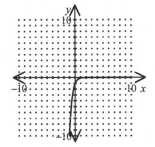

[D]

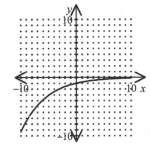

Lesson 6: Exponential Functions

[8.6.2.50] *Dynamic Item*

50. Which is the graph of the function?

$$y = \left(\frac{1}{4}\right)^x$$

[A]

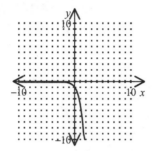

[B]

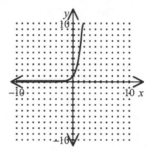

[C]

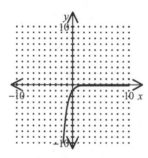

[D]

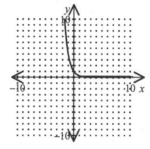

[8.6.2.51] *Dynamic Item*

51. Graph the function.
    $y = 0.8^x$.

[8.6.2.52] *Dynamic Item*

52. Graph the function.

$$y = \left(\frac{2}{3}\right)^x$$

Lesson 7: Applications of Exponential Functions

Objective 1: Use exponential functions to model applications that include growth and decay in different contexts.

[8.7.1.53] *Dynamic Item*

53. A boat that costs $8700 decreases in value by 12% per year. How much will the boat be worth after 3 years?

    [A] $3522.87   [B] $2771.19   [C] $5928.81   [D] $8664.00

[8.7.1.54] *Dynamic Item*

54. A certain species of animal is endangered and its numbers are decreasing at an annual rate of 21%. There are currently 380 animals in the population. Which is an exponential function representing the population and the estimated number of animals in 5 years?

    [A] $f(x) = 380(0.79)^x$; 1501   [B] $f(x) = 380(1.21)^x$; 986

    [C] $f(x) = 380(1.21)^x$; 2299   [D] $f(x) = 380(0.79)^x$; 117

[8.7.1.55] *Dynamic Item*

55. Use the table below to estimate the age of a sample in which 38% of the carbon-14 originally present still remains.

Years	0	5700	11,400	17,100	22,800	28,500	34,200
Carbon -14 remaining	1	$\dfrac{1}{2}$	$\dfrac{1}{4}$	$\dfrac{1}{8}$	$\dfrac{1}{16}$	$\dfrac{1}{32}$	$\dfrac{1}{64}$

[8.7.1.56] *Dynamic Item*

56. Use the formula $P = A(1+r)^t$, to determine the amount, A, that must be invested at 4.5%, compounded annually, so that $300,000 will be available for retirement in 15 years.

Lesson 1: Laws of Exponents: Multiplying Monomials

Objective 1: Define exponents and powers.

[8.1.1.1] *Dynamic Item*

[1] [B]

[8.1.1.2] *Dynamic Item*

[2] [C]

[8.1.1.3] *Dynamic Item*

[3] 1000

[8.1.1.4] *Dynamic Item*

[4] 614,400

Objective 2: Find products of powers.

[8.1.2.5] *Dynamic Item*

[5] [B]

[8.1.2.6] *Dynamic Item*

[6] [A]

[8.1.2.7] *Dynamic Item*

[7] b^7

[8.1.2.8] *Dynamic Item*

[8] 7^{15}

Objective 3: Simplify products of monomials.

[8.1.3.9] *Dynamic Item*

[9] [B]

[8.1.3.10] *Dynamic Item*

[10] [D]

[8.1.3.11] *Dynamic Item*

[11] $32x^7y^4$

[8.1.3.12] *Dynamic Item*

[12] $144xy^2$

Lesson 2: Laws of Exponents: Powers and Products

Objective 1: Find the power of a power.

[8.2.1.13] *Dynamic Item*

[13] [B]

[8.2.1.14] *Dynamic Item*

[14] [C]

[8.2.1.15] *Dynamic Item*

[15] 4096

[8.2.1.16] *Dynamic Item*

[16] c^{3y}

Algebra 1

Objective 2: Find the power of a product.

[8.2.2.17] *Dynamic Item*

[17] [C]

[8.2.2.18] *Dynamic Item*

[18] [C]

[8.2.2.19] *Dynamic Item*

[19] $16w^{10}x^{12}y^2$

[8.2.2.20] *Dynamic Item*

[20] 64,000

Lesson 3: Laws of Exponents: Dividing Monomials

Objective 1: Simplify quotients of powers.

[8.3.1.21] *Dynamic Item*

[21] [C]

[8.3.1.22] *Dynamic Item*

[22] [B]

[8.3.1.23] *Dynamic Item*

[23] $0.3d^4e^5$

[8.3.1.24] *Dynamic Item*

[24] 7^4 ; 2401

Objective 2: Simplify powers of fractions.

[8.3.2.25] *Dynamic Item*

[25] [D]

[8.3.2.26] *Dynamic Item*

[26] [D]

[8.3.2.27] *Dynamic Item*

[27] $\dfrac{1}{125}$

[8.3.2.28] *Dynamic Item*

[28] $\dfrac{4^c a^{2c} b^{5c}}{c^c}$

Lesson 4: Negative and Zero Exponents

Objective 1: Understand the concepts of negative and zero exponents.

[8.4.1.29] *Dynamic Item*

[29] [D]

[8.4.1.30] *Dynamic Item*

[30] [C]

[8.4.1.31] *Dynamic Item*

[31] $\dfrac{1}{10,000}$

[8.4.1.32] *Dynamic Item*

[32] $\dfrac{4}{x}$

Objective 2: Simplify expressions containing negative and zero exponents.

[8.4.2.33] *Dynamic Item*

[33] [D]

[8.4.2.34] *Dynamic Item*

[34] [D]

[8.4.2.35] *Dynamic Item*

[35] $\dfrac{a}{9b}$

[8.4.2.36] *Dynamic Item*

[36] $\dfrac{6a^3b^7}{c^{11}}$

Lesson 5: Scientific Notation

Objective 1: Recognize the need for special notation in scientific calculations.

[8.5.1.37] *Dynamic Item*

[37] [A]

[8.5.1.38] *Dynamic Item*

[38] [D]

[8.5.1.39] *Dynamic Item*

[39] 2.064×10^8

[8.5.1.40] *Dynamic Item*

[40] 7.3×10^3

Objective 2: Perform computations involving scientific notation.

[8.5.2.41] *Dynamic Item*

[41] [C]

[8.5.2.42] *Dynamic Item*

[42] [A]

[8.5.2.43] *Dynamic Item*

[43] 0.480 seconds

[8.5.2.44] *Dynamic Item*

[44] 6.3×10^{14}

Lesson 6: Exponential Functions

Objective 1: Understand exponential functions and how they are used.

[8.6.1.45] *Dynamic Item*

[45] [B]

[8.6.1.46] *Dynamic Item*

[46] [B]

[8.6.1.47] *Dynamic Item*

[47] $2910

[8.6.1.48] *Dynamic Item*

[48] $P = 290(1.15)^x$; 583

Objective 2: Recognize differences between graphs of exponential functions with different bases.

[8.6.2.49] *Dynamic Item*

[49] [A]

[8.6.2.50] *Dynamic Item*

[50] [D]

[8.6.2.51] *Dynamic Item*

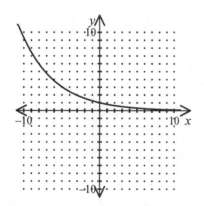

[51]

[8.6.2.52] *Dynamic Item*

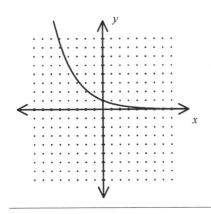

[52] _____

Lesson 7: Applications of Exponential Functions

Objective 1: Use exponential functions to model applications that include growth and decay in different contexts.

[8.7.1.53] *Dynamic Item*

[53] [C]

[8.7.1.54] *Dynamic Item*

[54] [D]

[8.7.1.55] *Dynamic Item*

[55] 8000 years (answers may vary due to estimation)

[8.7.1.56] *Dynamic Item*

[56] $155,016.13

Algebra 1
167

Lesson 1: Adding and Subtracting Polynomials

Objective 1: Add and subtract polynomials.

[9.1.1.1] *Dynamic Item*

1. Find the sum or difference.
    $$\left(4x^2 + x + 2\right) + \left(-2x^2 - 8\right)$$

    [A] $6x^2 + x - 6$ [B] $2x^2 + x - 6$ [C] $2x^2 + x + 10$ [D] $6x^2 + x + 10$

[9.1.1.2] *Dynamic Item*

2. Find the sum or difference.
    $$\left(3x^2 - 3x^4 + 3\right) - \left(-7x^4 + 5 - 7x^2\right)$$

    [A] $-4x^4 + 2x^2 - 2$ [B] $-4x^4 + 2x^2 - 4$ [C] $4x^4 + 10x^2 + 6$ [D] $4x^4 + 10x^2 - 2$

[9.1.1.3] *Dynamic Item*

3. Find the sum or difference.
    $$3x^2 - 4x - 5$$
    $$- \quad \left(-8x^2 - 7x - 3\right)$$

[9.1.1.4] *Dynamic Item*

4. Write the polynomial $2x^2 - 2x + 8x^3 + 2$ in standard form. Name the polynomial by the number of terms and by degree.

Lesson 2: Modeling Polynomial Multiplication

Objective 1: Use algebra tiles to model the products of binomials.

[9.2.1.5] *Dynamic Item*

5. White algebra tiles represent positive numbers and black algebra tiles represent negative numbers. What product of binomial factors is represented by the model shown?

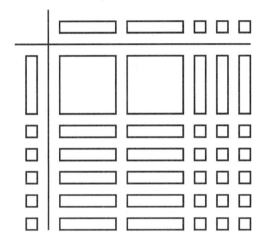

[A] $(2x+3)(x+5) = 2x^2 + 13x + 15$ [B] $(2x^2 + 3x)(x^2 + 5x) = 2x^2 + 15x$

[C] $(2x+3)(x+5) = 2x^2 + 15$ [D] $(2x+3)(x+5) = 2x^2 + 15x + 15$

[9.2.1.6] *Dynamic Item*

6. White algebra tiles represent positive numbers and black algebra tiles represent negative numbers. What product of binomial factors is represented by the model shown?

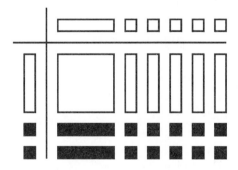

[A] $(x+5)(x+2) = x^2 - 7x - 10$ [B] $(x-5)(x+2) = x^2 - 3x - 10$

[C] $(x+5)(x-2) = x^2 + 3x - 10$ [D] $(x+5)(x+2) = x^2 + 3x - 10$

Lesson 2: Modeling Polynomial Multiplication

[9.2.1.7] *Dynamic Item*

7. White algebra tiles represent positive numbers and black algebra tiles represent negative numbers. Model the product $(x+2)(x+1)$ with algebra tiles and give the simplified product.

[9.2.1.8] *Dynamic Item*

8. White algebra tiles represent positive numbers and black algebra tiles represent negative numbers. What product of binomial factors is represented by the model shown?

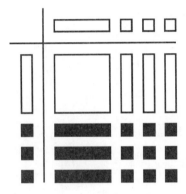

Objective 2: Mentally simplify special products of binomials.

[9.2.2.9] *Dynamic Item*

9. Find the product by using the rules for special products.
   $(5u+9)(5u-9)$

   [A] $25u^2 - 81$ [B] $25u^2 + 45u - 81$ [C] $25u^2 + 90u - 81$ [D] $25u^2 - 90u - 81$

[9.2.2.10] *Dynamic Item*

10. Find the product by using the rules for special products.
   $(2x+6)^2$

   [A] $4x^2 + 24x + 36$ [B] $4x^2 + 16x + 36$ [C] $4x^2 + 12x + 36$ [D] $4x^2 + 36$

Lesson 2: Modeling Polynomial Multiplication

[9.2.2.11] *Dynamic Item*

11. Find the product by using the rules for special products.
    $(2f+3)(2f-3)$

[9.2.2.12] *Dynamic Item*

12. Find the product by using the rules for special products.
    $(5x+3)^2$

Lesson 3: Multiplying Binomials

Objective 1: Find products of binomials using the Distributive Property.

[9.3.1.13] *Dynamic Item*

13. Use the Distributive Property to find each product.
    $(4x-7)(3x-4)$

    [A] $12x^2-37x+28$ [B] $12x^2+37x+28$

    [C] $12x^2-37x-28$ [D] $12x^2+5x+28$

[9.3.1.14] *Dynamic Item*

14. Use the Distributive Property to find each product.
    $(x-5)(x+3)$

    [A] $x^2-2x-15$ [B] $x^2+8x-15$ [C] $x^2-8x-15$ [D] $x^2-2x+15$

[9.3.1.15] *Dynamic Item*

15. Use the Distributive Property to find each product.
    $3x(x^3-5)$

Lesson 3: Multiplying Binomials

[9.3.1.16] *Dynamic Item*

16. A flower bed has a brick walkway surrounding it. What is the area of the flower bed, including the walkway?

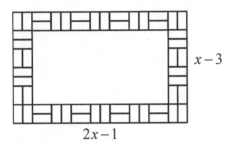

Objective 2: Find products of binomials by using the FOIL method.

[9.3.2.17] *Dynamic Item*

17. Use the FOIL method to find the product.
$(x^2 - 9)(x^2 + 4)$

[A] $x^2 - 13x - 36$ [B] $x^4 - 5x^2 - 36$ [C] $x^4 - 36x^2 + 13$ [D] $x^2 - 5x^2 - 36$

[9.3.2.18] *Dynamic Item*

18. Use the FOIL method to find the product.
$(3.5x + 8)(2.0x + 2)$

[A] $7.00x^2 - 24.0x + 16$ [B] $7.00x^2 + 23.0x + 16$

[C] $7.00x^2 + 23.0x + 17$ [D] $7.00x^2 - 9.0x + 17$

[9.3.2.19] *Dynamic Item*

19. Use the FOIL method to find the product.
$(9x + 8)(9x + 2)$

Lesson 3: Multiplying Binomials

[9.3.2.20] *Dynamic Item*

20. Use the FOIL method to find the product.

$$\left(h-\frac{2}{3}\right)\left(h+\frac{1}{4}\right)$$

Lesson 4: Polynomial Functions

Objective 1: Define polynomial functions.

[9.4.1.21] *Dynamic Item*

21. Use the table of values to select the polynomial function which has the same values for $x=1$ and $x=10$ as $f(x)=x^2-49$.

x	$f(x)=x^2-49$
1	-48
10	51

[A] $g(x)=(x+7)(x-9)$ [B] $g(x)=(x+7)(x-7)$

[C] $g(x)=(x+7)(x+7)$ [D] $g(x)=(x-7)(x-7)$

[9.4.1.22] *Dynamic Item*

22. Which of the following is *not* a polynomial function?

[A] $f(x)=3x^6-x^3+4x+3$ [B] $f(x)=x^6+\frac{1}{7}x^3+2$

[C] $f(x)=\frac{x+3}{2}-\frac{x}{2}$ [D] $f(x)=\frac{1}{3}x^5+\frac{x^{-3}}{4}$

Lesson 4: Polynomial Functions

[9.4.1.23] *Dynamic Item*

23. Complete the table to verify the equation is an identity: $x^3 - 125 = (x-5)(x^2 + 5x + 25)$

x	$f(x) = x^3 - 125$	$g(x) = (x-5)(x^2 + 5x + 25)$
-3		
-2		
-1		
0		
1		
2		
3		

[9.4.1.24] *Dynamic Item*

24. Tell whether $f(x) = 2x^4 - x^3 - \dfrac{4}{x}$ is a polynomial function. Explain.

Lesson 4: Polynomial Functions

Objective 2: Solve problems involving polynomial functions.

[9.4.2.25] *Dynamic Item*

25. The GREAT TASTE cereal company wants to increase the size of their containers by 30%. The present container is a cylinder with a diameter of 12 centimeters and a height of 18 centimeters. For the new package, the diameter will remain the same, but the height will change. What are the height and volume of the new package? The volume of a cylinder is $V = \pi r^2 h$, where r is the radius and h is the height.

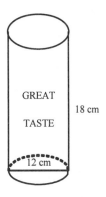

[A] The new volume is 6280 cm^3 and the new height is 22.1 cm.

[B] The new volume is 6280 cm^3 and the new height is 23.4 cm.

[C] The new volume is 2645.1 cm^3 and the new height is 23.4 cm.

[D] The new volume is 2645.1 cm^3 and the new height is 22.1 cm.

[9.4.2.26] *Dynamic Item*

26. Find the surface area of a cube with an edge of $2v$ centimeters.

[A] $24v^2$ cm^2 [B] $8v^2$ cm^2 [C] $6v^2$ cm^2 [D] $12v^2$ cm^2

[9.4.2.27] *Dynamic Item*

27. Find the volume of a rectangular prism with edges of $3z$, $5z$ and $4z$ centimeters.

Lesson 4: Polynomial Functions

[9.4.2.28] *Dynamic Item*

28. Complete the table for each given radius. Round your answers to the nearest tenth.

Radius r	Circumference $C = 2\pi r$	Surface Area $A = 4\pi r^2$	Volume $A = \dfrac{4\pi r^3}{3}$
0.4 inch			
11 inches			

Lesson 5: Common Factors

Objective 1: Factor a polynomial by using the greatest common factor.

[9.5.1.29] *Dynamic Item*

29. Factor the polynomial.
$x^2 - x^4$

[A] $x^2(1 - x^2)$ [B] $x^2(1 - 2x)$ [C] $x^2(x^2 - x)$ [D] $x^2(x^2 - 2x)$

[9.5.1.30] *Dynamic Item*

30. Factor the polynomial.
$6x^2 - 21x$

[A] $3x(2x - 7)$ [B] $6x - 21$ [C] $-15x$ [D] $x(6x - 21)$

[9.5.1.31] *Dynamic Item*

31. Factor the polynomial.
$30x^3 - 35x^2 + 10x$

Lesson 5: Common Factors

[9.5.1.32] *Dynamic Item*

32. Factor the polynomial.
$40x + 5$

Objective 2: Factor a polynomial by using a binomial factor.

[9.5.2.33] *Dynamic Item*

33. Which is the polynomial written as the product of two binomials?
$3x(x+4)+5(x+4)$

[A] $(3x+4)(x+5)$ [B] $3+(x+5)(x+4)$

[C] $x(3x+4)+20$ [D] $(3x+5)(x+4)$

[9.5.2.34] *Dynamic Item*

34. Which is the polynomial written as the product of two binomials?
$7x^3 - 14x^2 + x - 2$

[A] $(x-2)(7x^2+1)$ [B] $7x^2(x-2)$ [C] $(x-14)(7x^2-1)$ [D] $x(7x^2-2x-2)$

[9.5.2.35] *Dynamic Item*

35. Write the polynomial as the product of two binomials.
$3x(x-7)-8(x-7)$

[9.5.2.36] *Dynamic Item*

36. Write the polynomial as the product of two binomials.
$14pz - 21z - 10py + 15y$

Lesson 6: Factoring Special Polynomials

Objective 1: Factor perfect-square trinomials.

[9.6.1.37] *Dynamic Item*

37. Factor the polynomial completely.
$c^2 - 12c + 36$

[A] $(c-36)(c+1)$ [B] $(c+6)^2$ [C] $(c-6)(c+6)$ [D] $(c-6)^2$

[9.6.1.38] *Dynamic Item*

38. Factor the polynomial completely.
$100x^2 - 140xy + 49y^2$

[A] $(10x+7y)^2$ [B] $(10x-7y)(10x+7y)$

[C] $(100x-7y)(x+7y)$ [D] $(10x-7y)^2$

[9.6.1.39] *Dynamic Item*

39. Factor the polynomial completely.
$25q^2 - 20qr + 4r^2$

[9.6.1.40] *Dynamic Item*

40. Factor the polynomial completely.
$25x^2 + 20x + 4$

Objective 2: Factor the difference of two squares.

[9.6.2.41] *Dynamic Item*

41. Factor the polynomial completely.
$x^2 - 36$

[A] $(x+6)(x-6)$ [B] $(x+6)(x+6)$ [C] $(x-6)(x-6)$ [D] $(x+6)(x-4)$

Lesson 6: Factoring Special Polynomials

[9.6.2.42] *Dynamic Item*

42. Factor the polynomial completely.
    $25x^2 - 64y^2$

    [A] $(5x - 8y)^2$ [B] $(5x + 8)(5x - 8)$ [C] $(5x + 8y)^2$ [D] $(5x + 8y)(5x - 8y)$

[9.6.2.43] *Dynamic Item*

43. Factor the polynomial completely.
    $81x^2 - 25$

[9.6.2.44] *Dynamic Item*

44. Factor the polynomial completely.
    $256x^4 - y^4$

Lesson 7: Factoring Quadratic Trinomials

Objective 1: Factor quadratic trinomials by using algebra tiles.

[9.7.1.45] *Dynamic Item*

45. Black algebra tiles represent negative numbers and white algebra tiles represent positive numbers. Rearrange the algebra tiles shown into a rectangle and show the area of the rectangle as the product of its dimensions. You may need to add neutral pairs.

$x^2 - x - 12$

    [A] $(x + 3)(x - 4)$ [B] $(x - 3)(x - 4)$ [C] $(x + 4)(x - 3)$ [D] $(x - 1)(x - 3)$

Lesson 7: Factoring Quadratic Trinomials

[9.7.1.46] *Dynamic Item*

46. Black algebra tiles represent negative numbers and white algebra tiles represent positive numbers. Rearrange the algebra tiles shown into a rectangle and show the area of the rectangle as the product of its dimensions. You may need to add neutral pairs.

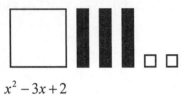

$x^2 - 3x + 2$

[A] $(x+1)(x+2)$ [B] $(x-3)(x+2)$ [C] $(x-2)(x+1)$ [D] $(x-1)(x-2)$

[9.7.1.47] *Dynamic Item*

47. Use algebra tiles to factor the given trinomial.
$x^2 - x - 6$

[9.7.1.48] *Dynamic Item*

48. Use algebra tiles to factor the given trinomial.
$x^2 - 4x + 3$

Objective 2: Factor quadratic trinomials by using guess-and-check methods.

[9.7.2.49] *Dynamic Item*

49. Factor the polynomial completely.
$x^2 - 7x - 18$

[A] $(x+7)(x-6)$ [B] $(x-9)(x+2)$ [C] $(x-7)(x+6)$ [D] $(x+9)(x-2)$

Lesson 7: Factoring Quadratic Trinomials

[9.7.2.50] *Dynamic Item*

50. Factor the polynomial completely.
$$-2x^4y^4 + 18$$

[A] $(x^3y^3 - 3)(-2xy - 6)$ [B] $-2(x^2y^2 - 3)(x^2y^2 + 3)$

[C] $-4(x^4y^4 + 9)$ [D] $-2(x^2y^2 - 3)^2$

[9.7.2.51] *Dynamic Item*

51. Factor the polynomial completely.
$$7x^3 - 21x^2 + x - 3$$

[9.7.2.52] *Dynamic Item*

52. Factor the polynomial completely.
$$3x^3 - 6x^2 - 9x$$

Lesson 8: Solving Equations by Factoring

Objective 1: Solve equations by factoring.

[9.8.1.53] *Dynamic Item*

53. Solve by factoring: $x^2 - 2x - 24 = 0$

[A] $x = 4$ or $x = 6$ [B] $x = -4$ or $x = 6$

[C] $x = -4$ or $x = -6$ [D] $x = 4$ or $x = -6$

[9.8.1.54] *Dynamic Item*

54. Identify the zeros of the function: $y = (x - 6)(x - 9)$

[A] $x = 6$ and $x = -9$ [B] $x = -6$ and $x = 9$

[C] $x = 6$ and $x = 9$ [D] $x = -6$ and $x = -9$

Lesson 8: Solving Equations by Factoring

[9.8.1.55] *Dynamic Item*

55. Solve by factoring: $x^2 - 11x = -24$

[9.8.1.56] *Dynamic Item*

56. A farmer has 760 feet of fencing available and wishes to enclose a rectangular area. Complete the table of values to show the length, width and area of these possible pens. Which pen has the largest area?

Perimeter	Length	Width	Area
760	215		
760	190		
760	165		

Lesson 1: Adding and Subtracting Polynomials

Objective 1: Add and subtract polynomials.

[9.1.1.1] *Dynamic Item*

[1] [B]

[9.1.1.2] *Dynamic Item*

[2] [D]

[9.1.1.3] *Dynamic Item*

[3] $11x^2 + 3x - 2$

[9.1.1.4] *Dynamic Item*

$8x^3 + 2x^2 - 2x + 2$
[4] polynomial; cubic

Lesson 2: Modeling Polynomial Multiplication

Objective 1: Use algebra tiles to model the products of binomials.

[9.2.1.5] *Dynamic Item*

[5] [A]

[9.2.1.6] *Dynamic Item*

[6] [C]

[9.2.1.7] *Dynamic Item*

$x^2 + 3x + 2$

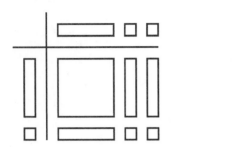

[7] _____

[9.2.1.8] *Dynamic Item*

[8] $(x+3)(x-3) = x^2 - 9$ _____

Objective 2: Mentally simplify special products of binomials.

[9.2.2.9] *Dynamic Item*

[9] [A] _____

[9.2.2.10] *Dynamic Item*

[10] [A] _____

[9.2.2.11] *Dynamic Item*

[11] $4f^2 - 9$ _____

[9.2.2.12] *Dynamic Item*

[12] $25x^2 + 30x + 9$ _____

Lesson 3: Multiplying Binomials

Objective 1: Find products of binomials using the Distributive Property.

[9.3.1.13] *Dynamic Item*

[13] [A]

[9.3.1.14] *Dynamic Item*

[14] [A]

[9.3.1.15] *Dynamic Item*

[15] $3x^4 - 15x$

[9.3.1.16] *Dynamic Item*

[16] $2x^2 - 7x + 3$ square feet

Objective 2: Find products of binomials by using the FOIL method.

[9.3.2.17] *Dynamic Item*

[17] [B]

[9.3.2.18] *Dynamic Item*

[18] [B]

[9.3.2.19] *Dynamic Item*

[19] $81x^2 + 90x + 16$

[9.3.2.20] *Dynamic Item*

[20] $h^2 - \dfrac{5}{12}h - \dfrac{1}{6}$

Lesson 4: Polynomial Functions

Objective 1: Define polynomial functions.

[9.4.1.21] *Dynamic Item*

[21] [B]

[9.4.1.22] *Dynamic Item*

[22] [D]

[9.4.1.23] *Dynamic Item*

x	$f(x)=x^3-125$	$g(x)=(x-5)(x^2+5x+25)$
-3	-152	-152
-2	-133	-133
-1	-126	-126
0	-125	-125
1	-124	-124
2	-117	-117
3	-98	-98

[23]

[9.4.1.24] *Dynamic Item*

[24] No. A polynomial function is the sum or difference of monomials. A monomial does not have a variable in the denominator.

Objective 2: Solve problems involving polynomial functions.

[9.4.2.25] *Dynamic Item*

[25] [C]

[9.4.2.26] *Dynamic Item*

[26] [A]

[9.4.2.27] *Dynamic Item*

[27] $60z^3$ cm^3

[9.4.2.28] *Dynamic Item*

Radius r	Circumference $C = 2\pi r$	Surface Area $A = 4\pi r^2$	Volume $A = \dfrac{4\pi r^3}{3}$
0.4 inch	2.5 in.	2 in^2	0.3 in^3
11 inches	69.1 in.	1520.5 in^2	5575.3 in^3

[28]

Lesson 5: Common Factors

Objective 1: Factor a polynomial by using the greatest common factor.

[9.5.1.29] *Dynamic Item*

[29] [A]

[9.5.1.30] *Dynamic Item*

[30] [A]

[9.5.1.31] *Dynamic Item*

[31] $5x(6x^2 - 7x + 2)$

[9.5.1.32] *Dynamic Item*

[32] $5(8x + 1)$

Objective 2: Factor a polynomial by using a binomial factor.

[9.5.2.33] *Dynamic Item*

[33] [D]

[9.5.2.34] *Dynamic Item*

[34] [A]

[9.5.2.35] *Dynamic Item*

[35] $(3x-8)(x-7)$

[9.5.2.36] *Dynamic Item*

[36] $(2p-3)(7z-5y)$

Lesson 6: Factoring Special Polynomials

Objective 1: Factor perfect-square trinomials.

[9.6.1.37] *Dynamic Item*

[37] [D]

[9.6.1.38] *Dynamic Item*

[38] [D]

[9.6.1.39] *Dynamic Item*

[39] $(5q-2r)^2$

[9.6.1.40] *Dynamic Item*

[40] $(5x+2)^2$

Objective 2: Factor the difference of two squares.

[9.6.2.41] *Dynamic Item*

[41] [A]

[9.6.2.42] *Dynamic Item*

[42] [D]

[9.6.2.43] *Dynamic Item*

[43] $(9x-5)(9x+5)$

[9.6.2.44] *Dynamic Item*

[44] $(4x-y)(4x+y)(16x^2+y^2)$

Lesson 7: Factoring Quadratic Trinomials

Objective 1: Factor quadratic trinomials by using algebra tiles.

[9.7.1.45] *Dynamic Item*

[45] [A]

[9.7.1.46] *Dynamic Item*

[46] [D]

[9.7.1.47] *Dynamic Item*

$(x+2)(x-3)$

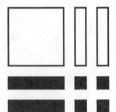

[47] _____

[9.7.1.48] *Dynamic Item*

$(x-1)(x-3)$

[48] _____

Objective 2: Factor quadratic trinomials by using guess-and-check methods.

[9.7.2.49] *Dynamic Item*

[49] [B]

[9.7.2.50] *Dynamic Item*

[50] [B]

[9.7.2.51] *Dynamic Item*

[51] $(x-3)(7x^2+1)$

[9.7.2.52] *Dynamic Item*

[52] $3x(x+1)(x-3)$

Lesson 8: Solving Equations by Factoring

Objective 1: Solve equations by factoring.

[9.8.1.53] *Dynamic Item*

[53] [B]

[9.8.1.54] *Dynamic Item*

[54] [C]

[9.8.1.55] *Dynamic Item*

[55] $x=8$ or $x=3$

[9.8.1.56] *Dynamic Item*

Perimeter	Length	Width	Area
760	215	165	35,475
760	190	190	36,100
760	165	215	35,475

[56] The largest pen has 36,100 square feet of area.

Lesson 1: Graphing Parabolas

Objective 1: Discover how adding a constant to the parent function $y = x^2$ affects the graph of the function.

[10.1.1.1] *Dynamic Item*

1. Identify the vertex and the axis of symmetry for the graph of $y = -4(x-5)^2 + 3$.

   [A] vertex (5, 3); $x = 5$ [B] vertex (–5, –3); $x = 5$

   [C] vertex (–5, –3); $x = -5$ [D] vertex (5, 3); $x = -5$

[10.1.1.2] *Dynamic Item*

2. Which is the graph of $y = (x+1)^2 - 4$?

   [A] 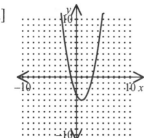   [B]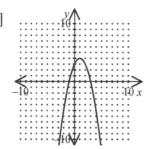

   [C] 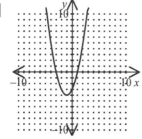   [D]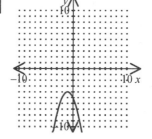

[10.1.1.3] *Dynamic Item*

3. Graph $y = -3(x-1)^2 - 5$. Identify the vertex and the axis of symmetry.

Algebra 1

192

Lesson 1: Graphing Parabolas

[10.1.1.4] *Dynamic Item*

4. Find the rule and the graph of the function whose graph can be obtained by performing the translation 3 units left and 4 units down on the parent function $f(x) = x^2$.

Objective 2: Use the zeros of a quadratic function to find the vertex of the graph of the function.

[10.1.2.5] *Dynamic Item*

5. Which is the vertex of the graph of $y = x^2 + 10x + 21$?

   [A] $(-7, -3)$ [B] $(3, 7)$ [C] $(-5, -4)$ [D] $(5, 4)$

[10.1.2.6] *Dynamic Item*

6. Use factoring to find the zeros of $y = x^2 + 6x + 5$ and the equation of the axis of symmetry.

   [A] $-5, -1; x = -3$ [B] $5, 1; x = 3$ [C] $-5, -1; y = -3$ [D] $5, 1; y = 3$

[10.1.2.7] *Dynamic Item*

7. Use factoring to find the zeros of $y = x^2 + 13x + 42$ and the equation of the axis of symmetry.

[10.1.2.8] *Dynamic Item*

8. Use the zeros to find the vertex of the graph of $y = x^2 + 2x - 15$ and write the vertex form of the quadratic function.

Lesson 2: Solving Equations by Using Square Roots

Objective 1: Solve equations of the form $ax^2 = k$.

[10.2.1.9] *Dynamic Item*

9. Solve the equation. Round answers to the nearest hundredth when necessary.
   $x^2 = 180$

   [A] −12.92, 12.92   [B] −90, 90   [C] −13.42, 13.42   [D] 13.42

[10.2.1.10] *Dynamic Item*

10. Solve the equation. Round answers to the nearest hundredth when necessary.
    $3x^2 = 48$

    [A] ± 8 [B] ± 6.93 [C] ± 0.25 [D] ± 4

[10.2.1.11] *Dynamic Item*

11. Solve the equation. Round answers to the nearest hundredth when necessary.
    $64x^2 = 9$

[10.2.1.12] *Dynamic Item*

12. Solve the equation. Round answers to the nearest hundredth when necessary.
    $x^2 = 4$

Objective 2: Solve equations of the form $x^2 = k$ where x is replaced by an algebraic expression.

[10.2.2.13] *Dynamic Item*

13. Solve the equation. Round answers to the nearest hundredth when necessary.
    $4(x+3)^2 = 9$

    [A] 1.5 and −4.5   [B] 0 and −6   [C] −1.5 and 4.5   [D] −1.5, −4.5

Lesson 2: Solving Equations by Using Square Roots

[10.2.2.14] *Dynamic Item*

14. Solve the equation. Round answers to the nearest hundredth when necessary.
    $(x+1)^2 = 67$

    [A] $-9.19, -7.19$ [B] $9.19, -7.19$ [C] $-9.19, 7.19$ [D] $9.19, 7.19$

[10.2.2.15] *Dynamic Item*

15. Solve the equation. Round answers to the nearest hundredth when necessary.
    $(x-5)^2 = 64$

[10.2.2.16] *Dynamic Item*

16. The equation that describes the path of a small rocket after it is shot into the air is
    $h = 1408 - 16t^2$, where h is the height above the ground, in feet, after t seconds. How many
    seconds does it take for the rocket to return to the ground?

Lesson 3: Completing the Square

Objective 1: Form a perfect-square trinomial from a given quadratic binomial.

[10.3.1.17] *Dynamic Item*

17. Which of the following values of k makes the polynomial a perfect square?
    $x^2 + 19x + k$

    [A] 361   [B] $\dfrac{361}{4}$ [C] $\dfrac{2}{361}$ [D] $\dfrac{361}{2}$

[10.3.1.18] *Dynamic Item*

18. Find the number and the binomial which could be inserted in the blanks to make the
    equation true.
    $x^2 + 12x + \underline{\hspace{2em}} = (\underline{\hspace{2em}})^2$

    [A] $36; x+6$ [B] $36; x-6$ [C] $12; x+12$ [D] $12; x-12$

Lesson 3: Completing the Square

[10.3.1.19] *Dynamic Item*

19. Find the number and the binomial which could be inserted in the blanks to make the
equation true.

$$x^2 - 8x + \underline{\hspace{2cm}} = (\underline{\hspace{1.5cm}})^2$$

[10.3.1.20] *Dynamic Item*

20. Which number must be added to $x^2 - 10x$ to make it a perfect square trinomial?

Objective 2: Write a given quadratic function in vertex form.

[10.3.2.21] *Dynamic Item*

21. Which of the following is the given function rewritten in vertex form?
$$y = x^2 + 10x + 25 - 25$$

[A] $y = (x+10)^2 - 25$ [B] $y = (x-10)^2 - 25$

[C] $y = (x-5)^2 - 25$ [D] $y = (x+5)^2 - 25$

[10.3.2.22] *Dynamic Item*

22. Which of the following is the given function rewritten in vertex form?
$$y = x^2 - 1$$

[A] $y = (x+1)^2 - 1$ [B] $y = (x-1)^2 + 0$ [C] $y = (x-0)^2 - 1$ [D] $y = (x+1)^2 + 0$

[10.3.2.23] *Dynamic Item*

23. Write the given function in vertex form.
$$y = x^2 + 4x$$

Lesson 3: Completing the Square

[10.3.2.24] *Dynamic Item*

24. Write the given function in vertex form.
$$y = x^2 + 8x + 4$$

Lesson 4: Solving Equations of the Form $x^2 + bx + c = 0$

Objective 1: Solve quadratic equations by completing the square or by factoring.

[10.4.1.25] *Dynamic Item*

25. Which are the solutions to the given equation? Answers are rounded to the nearest hundredth when necessary.
$$x^2 + 6x - 7 = 0$$

[A] –6, 7   [B] 7, –1   [C] 6, –7   [D] –7, 1

[10.4.1.26] *Dynamic Item*

26. Which are the solutions to the given equation? Answers are rounded to the nearest hundredth when necessary.
$$x^2 + 5x = 0$$

[A] –5, –1   [B] –4, 0   [C] –5, 0   [D] –3, 0

[10.4.1.27] *Dynamic Item*

27. Solve the equation by factoring: $x^2 - 2x - 15 = 0$

[10.4.1.28] *Dynamic Item*

28. Solve by completing the square: $x^2 + 4x = 60$

Lesson 5: The Quadratic Formula

Objective 1: Use the quadratic formula to find solutions to quadratic equations.

[10.5.1.29] *Dynamic Item*

29. Use the quadratic formula to solve the equation. Give exact answers.
$$8x^2 + 2x - 15 = 0$$

[A] $-\dfrac{5}{4}, \dfrac{3}{2}$ [B] $\dfrac{5}{4}, -\dfrac{3}{2}$ [C] $\dfrac{5}{4}, \dfrac{3}{2}$ [D] $-\dfrac{5}{4}, -\dfrac{3}{2}$

[10.5.1.30] *Dynamic Item*

30. Use the quadratic formula to solve the equation. Give exact answers.
$$3x^2 - 1 = 5x$$

[A] $\dfrac{5 + \sqrt{13}}{6}, \dfrac{5 - \sqrt{13}}{6}$ [B] $\dfrac{-5 + \sqrt{13}}{6}, \dfrac{-5 - \sqrt{13}}{6}$

[C] $\dfrac{-5 + \sqrt{37}}{6}, \dfrac{-5 - \sqrt{37}}{6}$ [D] $\dfrac{5 + \sqrt{37}}{6}, \dfrac{5 - \sqrt{37}}{6}$

[10.5.1.31] *Dynamic Item*

31. Use the quadratic formula to solve the equation. Give exact answers.
$$3x^2 - 13x = 10$$

[10.5.1.32] *Dynamic Item*

32. Use the quadratic formula to solve the equation. Give exact answers.
$$x^2 + 6x + 3 = 0$$

Lesson 5: The Quadratic Formula

Objective 2: Use the quadratic formula to find the zeros of a quadratic function.

[10.5.2.33] *Dynamic Item*

33. Find the zeros of the function $y = 2x^2 + 15x + 18$.

[A] $\dfrac{3}{2}$, 6   [B] 1, $-\dfrac{17}{2}$ [C] -1, $\dfrac{17}{2}$ [D] $-\dfrac{3}{2}$, -6

[10.5.2.34] *Dynamic Item*

34. A rocket is launched from atop a 36-foot cliff with an initial velocity of 113 feet per second. The height of the rocket t seconds after launch is given by the equation $h = -16t^2 + 113t + 36$. Use the quadratic formula find out how long after the rocket is launched it will hit the ground ($h = 0$). Round your answer to the nearest tenth of a second.

[A] 7.4 sec   [B] 6.7 sec   [C] 0.3 sec   [D] 1.4 sec

[10.5.2.35] *Dynamic Item*

35. Find the exact zeros of the function.
$$y = -3x^2 - 3x - 3$$

[10.5.2.36] *Dynamic Item*

36. Find the exact zeros of the function.
$$y = x^2 + 2x - 1$$

Lesson 5: The Quadratic Formula

Objective 3: Evaluate the discriminant to determine how many real roots a quadratic equation has and whether it can be factored.

[10.5.3.37] *Dynamic Item*

37. Which of the following is the discriminant and the nature of the roots for $2x^2 + 2x - 4 = 0$?

   [A] The discriminant is –28 and there are two real roots.

   [B] The discriminant is 36 and there are two real roots.

   [C] The discriminant is –28 and there are no real roots.

   [D] The discriminant is 36 and there are no real roots.

[10.5.3.38] *Dynamic Item*

38. Use the quadratic formula to write $4x^2 - 25x - 21$ in factored form.

   [A] $(x-7)(4x-3)$ [B] $(4x+3)(x-7)$ [C] $(4x-3)(x+7)$ [D] $(4x+3)(x+7)$

[10.5.3.39] *Dynamic Item*

39. Find the discriminant of $5x^2 - 3x - 1 = 0$.

[10.5.3.40] *Dynamic Item*

40. Use the discriminant to find the number of real solutions to $2x^2 + 4x + 2 = 0$.

Lesson 6: Graphing Quadratic Inequalities

Objective 1: Solve and graph quadratic inequalities and test solution regions.

[10.6.1.41] *Dynamic Item*

41. Which is the correct graph of $y \leq -x^2 - 2x$?

[A]
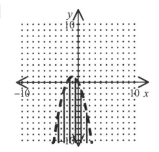

[B]
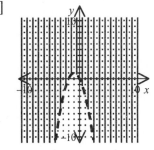

[C]
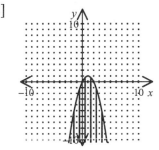

[D]
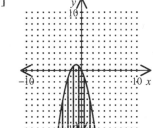

[10.6.1.42] *Dynamic Item*

42. Which is the graph of the solution for the quadratic inequality $x^2 - 2x \geq 15$?

[A]

[B]

[C]
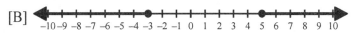

[D]

Lesson 6: Graphing Quadratic Inequalities

[10.6.1.43] *Dynamic Item*

43. Graph $y < -x^2 + 5$. Shade the solution region.

[10.6.1.44] *Dynamic Item*

44. The height of an arrow shot into the air is modeled by the equation $y = 176t - 16t^2$, where y is the height of the arrow above the ground in feet t seconds after it is released. Solve the quadratic inequality, $176t - 16t^2 > 384$, using the Zero Product Property, to find what period of time the arrow is above 384 feet.

Lesson 1: Graphing Parabolas

Objective 1: Discover how adding a constant to the parent function $y = x^2$ affects the graph of the function.

[10.1.1.1] *Dynamic Item*

[1] [A]

[10.1.1.2] *Dynamic Item*

[2] [C]

[10.1.1.3] *Dynamic Item*

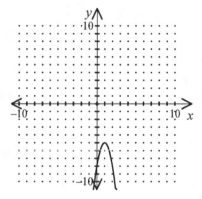

Vertex: $(1, -5)$

[3] Axis of symmetry: $x = 1$

[10.1.1.4] *Dynamic Item*

$$f(x) = (x+3)^2 - 4$$

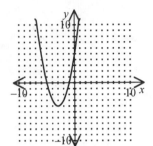

[4]

Objective 2: Use the zeros of a quadratic function to find the vertex of the graph of the function.

[10.1.2.5] *Dynamic Item*

[5] [C]

[10.1.2.6] *Dynamic Item*

[6] [A]

[10.1.2.7] *Dynamic Item*

[7] $-7, -6; \; x = -6.5$

[10.1.2.8] *Dynamic Item*

The zeros are –5, 3. The vertex is $(-1, -16)$. The vertex form of the equation is

[8] $y = (x+1)^2 - 16$.

Lesson 2: Solving Equations by Using Square Roots

Objective 1: Solve equations of the form $ax^2 = k$.

[10.2.1.9] *Dynamic Item*

[9] [C]

[10.2.1.10] *Dynamic Item*

[10] [D]

[10.2.1.11] *Dynamic Item*

[11] $-\dfrac{3}{8}, \dfrac{3}{8}$

[10.2.1.12] *Dynamic Item*

[12] ± 2

Objective 2: Solve equations of the form $x^2 = k$ where x is replaced by an algebraic expression.

[10.2.2.13] *Dynamic Item*

[13] [D]

[10.2.2.14] *Dynamic Item*

[14] [C]

[10.2.2.15] *Dynamic Item*

[15] $x = -3 \text{ or } x = 13$

[10.2.2.16] *Dynamic Item*

[16] 9.38 seconds

Lesson 3: Completing the Square

Objective 1: Form a perfect-square trinomial from a given quadratic binomial.

[10.3.1.17] *Dynamic Item*

[17] [B]

[10.3.1.18] *Dynamic Item*

[18] [A]

[10.3.1.19] *Dynamic Item*

[19] 16; $x - 4$

[10.3.1.20] *Dynamic Item*

[20] 25

Objective 2: Write a given quadratic function in vertex form.

[10.3.2.21] *Dynamic Item*

[21] [D]

[10.3.2.22] *Dynamic Item*

[22] [C]

[10.3.2.23] *Dynamic Item*

[23] $y = (x + 2)^2 - 4$

[10.3.2.24] *Dynamic Item*

[24] $y = (x + 4)^2 - 12$

Lesson 4: Solving Equations of the Form $x^2 + bx + c = 0$

Objective 1: Solve quadratic equations by completing the square or by factoring.

[10.4.1.25] *Dynamic Item*

[25] [D]

[10.4.1.26] *Dynamic Item*

[26] [C]

[10.4.1.27] *Dynamic Item*

[27] –3, 5

[10.4.1.28] *Dynamic Item*

[28] –10, 6

Lesson 5: The Quadratic Formula

Objective 1: Use the quadratic formula to find solutions to quadratic equations.

[10.5.1.29] *Dynamic Item*

[29] [B]

Algebra 1

[10.5.1.30] *Dynamic Item*

[30] [D]

[10.5.1.31] *Dynamic Item*

[31] $-\dfrac{2}{3}, 5$

[10.5.1.32] *Dynamic Item*

[32] $-3+\sqrt{6}, \ -3-\sqrt{6}$

Objective 2: Use the quadratic formula to find the zeros of a quadratic function.

[10.5.2.33] *Dynamic Item*

[33] [D]

[10.5.2.34] *Dynamic Item*

[34] [A]

[10.5.2.35] *Dynamic Item*

[35] No real solutions

[10.5.2.36] *Dynamic Item*

[36] $-1+\sqrt{2}, \ -1-\sqrt{2}$

Objective 3: Evaluate the discriminant to determine how many real roots a quadratic equation has and whether it can be factored.

[10.5.3.37] *Dynamic Item*

[37] [B]

[10.5.3.38] *Dynamic Item*

[38] [B]

[10.5.3.39] *Dynamic Item*

[39] 29

[10.5.3.40] *Dynamic Item*

[40] 1

Lesson 6: Graphing Quadratic Inequalities

Objective 1: Solve and graph quadratic inequalities and test solution regions.

[10.6.1.41] *Dynamic Item*

[41] [D]

[10.6.1.42] *Dynamic Item*

[42] [B]

[10.6.1.43] *Dynamic Item*

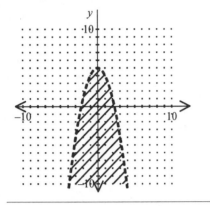

[43] _____

[10.6.1.44] *Dynamic Item*

[44] between 3 and 8 seconds _____

Lesson 1: Inverse Variation

Objective 1: Define and use two different forms of inverse variation to study real-world situations.

[11.1.1.1] *Dynamic Item*

1. If x varies inversely as y, and x is -50 when y is 42, which value is x when y is 70?

   [A] $x = -2100$ [B] $x = -30$ [C] $x = -147,000$ [D] $x = -59$

[11.1.1.2] *Dynamic Item*

2. Which of the following equations shows an inverse variation if $y = 4$ when $x = 3$?

   [A] $\dfrac{3}{4} = \dfrac{x}{y}$ [B] $xy = 12$ [C] $\dfrac{y}{4} = \dfrac{x}{3}$ [D] $\dfrac{y}{3} = \dfrac{x}{4}$

[11.1.1.3] *Dynamic Item*

3. A drama club is planning a bus trip to New York City to see a Broadway play. The cost per person for the bus rental varies inversely as the number of people going on the trip. It will cost $36 per person if 43 people go on the trip. How much will it cost per person if 100 people go on the trip?

[11.1.1.4] *Dynamic Item*

4. The time t required to drive a certain distance varies inversely as the speed r. If it takes 6 hours to drive the distance at 40 miles per hour, how long will it take to drive the same distance at 50 miles per hour?

Lesson 2: Rational Expressions and Functions

Objective 1: Define and illustrate the use of rational expressions and functions.

[11.2.1.5] *Dynamic Item*

5. For which value is the rational expression $\dfrac{x+5}{2x-3}$ undefined?

[A] $x = -\dfrac{3}{2}$ [B] $x = \dfrac{2}{3}$ [C] $x = -5$ [D] $x = \dfrac{3}{2}$

[11.2.1.6] *Dynamic Item*

6. Which is the graph of the rational function $y = -\dfrac{4}{x+3}$? Which is the undefined value?

[A]

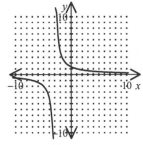

Undefined at $x = -3$.

[B]

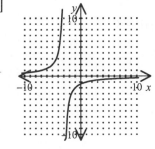

Undefined at $x = -3$.

[C]

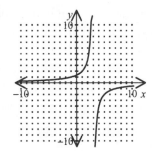

Undefined at $x = 3$.

[D]

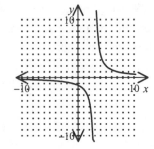

Undefined at $x = 3$.

Lesson 2: Rational Expressions and Functions

[11.2.1.7] *Dynamic Item*

7. Rewrite the function $y = \dfrac{30 - 6x}{6x}$ in simplest terms.

[11.2.1.8] *Dynamic Item*

8. Evaluate the function $y = \dfrac{x + 2}{x^2 - 2x - 3}$ at $x = -3$ and $x = -1$. Write *undefined* if appropriate.

Lesson 3: Simplifying Rational Expressions

Objective 1: Factor the numerator and denominator to simplify rational expressions.

[11.3.1.9] *Dynamic Item*

9. Simplify the expression.   [A] -1 [B] $\dfrac{x + 12}{x - 12}$ [C] $\dfrac{x + 4}{x - 4}$ [D] $\dfrac{x - 4}{x + 4}$
$$\dfrac{3x + 12}{3x - 12}$$

[11.3.1.10] *Dynamic Item*

10. Simplify the expression.
$$\dfrac{-12x + 18}{6}$$

[A] $-2x$ [B] $-2x + 3$ [C] $-24x + 3$ [D] $-2x + 18$

[11.3.1.11] *Dynamic Item*

11. Simplify the expression. State any restrictions on the variable.
$$\dfrac{7 - x}{x^2 + x - 56}$$

Lesson 3: Simplifying Rational Expressions

[11.3.1.12] *Dynamic Item*

12. Simplify the expression. State any restrictions on the variable.

$$\frac{x^2 - 5x + 6}{x^2 - 13x + 30}$$

Objective 2: State the restrictions on the variable of a simplified rational expression.

[11.3.2.13] *Dynamic Item*

13. For what value(s) of the variable is the expression undefined?

$$\frac{9}{t^2 + 5t}$$

[A] 0 or 5   [B] –5   [C] –5 or 0   [D] –5 or 5

[11.3.2.14] *Dynamic Item*

14. For what value(s) of the variable is the expression undefined?

$$\frac{x}{7 - x}$$

[A] 7   [B] –1   [C] 1   [D] –7

[11.3.2.15] *Dynamic Item*

15. For what value(s) of the variable is the expression undefined?

$$\frac{-1}{j^3 + 7j^2 - 18j}$$

[11.3.2.16] *Dynamic Item*

16. For what value(s) of the variable is the expression undefined?

$$\frac{p - 2}{p^2 - 6p + 8}$$

Lesson 3: Simplifying Rational Expressions

Objective 3: Extend simplification techniques to other algebraic fractions.

[11.3.3.17] *Dynamic Item*

17. Which of the following should be the result of the first step in simplifying the expression
$$\frac{3a^2 - 6b}{15x^2 + 30y}?$$

[A] $\dfrac{-3a^2 b}{15x^2 + 30y}$ [B] $\dfrac{3(a^2 - 2b)}{15(x^2 + 2y)}$ [C] $\dfrac{9a^2 - 6b}{225x^2 + 30y}$ [D] $\dfrac{3a^2 - 6b}{45x^2 y}$

[11.3.3.18] *Dynamic Item*

18. Simplify the expression.
$$\frac{-16(j^2 - k^2)}{4(j - k)}$$

[A] $-4(j - k)$ [B] $4(j + k)$ [C] $-4(j + k)$ [D] $4(j - k)$

[11.3.3.19] *Dynamic Item*

19. Simplify the expression.
$$\frac{2d + de}{3d}$$

[11.3.3.20] *Dynamic Item*

20. Simplify the expression.
$$\frac{8a^8 b^3}{64a^7 b^4}$$

Lesson 4: Operations With Rational Expressions

Objective 1: Perform operations with rational expressions in a real-world example.

[11.4.1.21] *Dynamic Item*

21. A speedboat travels at a rate of 2 times the speed of the current. Let x represent the speed of the current. Which of the following is an expression for t, the total time it takes the boat to travel 1 mile upstream and return the 1 mile downstream?

[A] $t = \dfrac{4}{3x}$ [B] $t = \dfrac{4}{9x}$ [C] $t = \dfrac{2}{3x}$ [D] $t = \dfrac{4}{x}$

[11.4.1.22] *Dynamic Item*

22. Amelia has been officially at bat 200 times and has hit 40 times. Her batting average is $\dfrac{40}{200} = 0.200$. How many consecutive hits must she get to increase her batting average to 0.500?

[A] 320   [B] 120   [C] 110   [D] none of these

[11.4.1.23] *Dynamic Item*

23. Ben Nordstrom is developing film in his darkroom when he realizes he does not have the proper developer. He needs a mixture that is 10% developer, but he only has a mixture that is 70% developer. How much pure water must be mixed with 8 pints of 70% developer to produce the mixture he needs? Round your answer to the nearest hundredth when necessary.

[11.4.1.24] *Dynamic Item*

24. Imagine that you own your own t-shirt business. The cost to have a silk screen artist design and set up the printing process is $350. In addition to this one-time charge, the cost of purchasing and printing each t-shirt is $6.25. Write a rational expression to find the average cost per shirt. Find the average cost per t-shirt when $x = 100$, 1000, and 10,000. What happens to the average cost per t-shirt as production level increases?

Lesson 4: Operations With Rational Expressions

Objective 2: Add, subtract, multiply, and divide rational expressions.

[11.4.2.25] *Dynamic Item*

25. Perform the indicated operation. Simplify and find the restrictions on the variable.

$$\frac{4}{x+8} + \frac{7}{x-8}$$

[A] $\dfrac{11}{(x+8)(x-8)}$; $x \neq \pm 8$

[B] $\dfrac{11}{x+8}$; $x \neq \pm 8$

[C] $\dfrac{11x+24}{11}$; $x \neq \pm 8$

[D] $\dfrac{11x+24}{(x+8)(x-8)}$; $x \neq \pm 8$

[11.4.2.26] *Dynamic Item*

26. Perform the indicated operation. Simplify and find the restrictions on the variable.

$$-\frac{6}{x^2-11x+30} - \frac{8}{x-6}$$

[A] $\dfrac{-8x-11}{x^2-11x+30}$; $x \neq -6,\ x \neq -5$

[B] $-\dfrac{14}{x^2-12x+36}$; $x \neq 6,\ x \neq -4$

[C] $\dfrac{-8x+34}{x^2-11x+30}$; $x \neq 6,\ x \neq 5$

[D] $\dfrac{-8x-46}{x^2-11x+30}$; $x \neq 6,\ x \neq 5$

[11.4.2.27] *Dynamic Item*

27. Perform the indicated operation. Simplify and state the restrictions on the variable.

$$\frac{n^2-16}{n+4} \cdot \frac{n}{5n-20}$$

[11.4.2.28] *Dynamic Item*

28. Perform the indicated operation. Simplify and state the restrictions on the variable.

$$\frac{x+7}{x-7} \div \frac{x^2-49}{7-x}$$

Lesson 5: Solving Rational Equations

Objective 1: Solve rational equations by using the common-denominator method.

[11.5.1.29] *Dynamic Item*

29. Solve the rational equation by using the lowest common denominator.

$$-\frac{1}{x}+\frac{9}{2x}=2$$

[A] $x=\dfrac{5}{3}$ [B] $x=\dfrac{7}{4}$ [C] $x=\dfrac{3}{5}$ [D] no solution

[11.5.1.30] *Dynamic Item*

30. Solve the rational equation by using the lowest common denominator.

$$\frac{x-2}{x-6}=\frac{x-5}{x-3}$$

[A] $x=3$ [B] $x=6$ [C] $x=4$ [D] $x=5$

[11.5.1.31] *Dynamic Item*

31. Solve the rational equation by using the lowest common denominator.

$$\frac{x}{x^2-4}+\frac{2}{x-2}=\frac{1}{x+2}$$

[11.5.1.32] *Dynamic Item*

32. Solve the rational equation by using the lowest common denominator.

$$\frac{x}{x+7}-\frac{1}{8}=\frac{-7}{x+7}$$

Lesson 5: Solving Rational Equations

Objective 2: Solve rational equations by graphing.

[11.5.2.33] *Dynamic Item*

33. Solve the rational equation by graphing.
$$\frac{7}{x} + \frac{1}{2} = \frac{4}{x}$$

[A] $x = -6$ [B] $x = 6$ [C] $x = 22$ [D] $x = 2$

[11.5.2.34] *Dynamic Item*

34. Solve the rational equation by graphing.
$$\frac{42 + x}{x} = x$$

[A] $x = -6$ or 5 [B] $x = -6$ or 7 [C] $x = -7$ or 6 [D] $x = 6$ or 7

[11.5.2.35] *Dynamic Item*

35. Solve the rational equation by graphing.
$$\frac{x - 6}{x - 4} = \frac{x - 2}{x - 4}$$

[11.5.2.36] *Dynamic Item*

36. Solve the rational equation by graphing.
$$\frac{2}{x - 4} - \frac{9}{x^2 - 4x} = 1$$

Lesson 6: Proof in Algebra

Objective 1: Define the parts of a conditional statement.

[11.6.1.37] *Dynamic Item*

37. Which is the hypothesis of the following conditional statement?
    "If a number is divisible by 5, then the last digit of the number is 0."

    [A] The last digit of the number is not 0.

    [B] A number is divisible by 5.

    [C] The last digit of the number is 0.

    [D] If a number is divisible by 5, then the last digit of the number is 0.

[11.6.1.38] *Dynamic Item*

38. Which is the conclusion of the following conditional statement?
    "If a number is even, then it is divisible by 6."

    [A] A number is not divisible by 6.

    [B] A number is divisible by 6.

    [C] If a number is even, then it is divisible by 6.

    [D] A number is even.

[11.6.1.39] *Dynamic Item*

39. Identify the hypothesis and conclusion of the conditional statement.
    "If the last digit of a number is 0, then it is divisible by 2."

[11.6.1.40] *Dynamic Item*

40. Identify the hypothesis and conclusion of the conditional statement.
    If $8x < 24$, then $x < 3$.

Lesson 6: Proof in Algebra

Objective 2: Define converse.

[11.6.2.41] *Dynamic Item*

41. You are asked to prove the converse of the statement: If n^2 is odd then n is odd . Which of the following statements is the conclusion of the conditional you must prove?

[A] n^2 is not odd   [B] n is not odd   [C] n is odd   [D] n^2 is odd

[11.6.2.42] *Dynamic Item*

42. You are asked to prove the converse of the statement: If n is even then n^2 is even. Which of the following statements is the hypothesis of the conditional you must prove?

[A] n^2 is odd   [B] n^2 is even   [C] n is odd   [D] n is even

[11.6.2.43] *Dynamic Item*

43. Write the converse: If a number is divisible by 9, then the sum of the digits of the number is divisible by 9.

[11.6.2.44] *Dynamic Item*

44. Determine if the conditional statement "If n^2 is odd , then n is odd ." is true. Then, write the converse of the statement and determine whether it is true.

Lesson 6: Proof in Algebra

Objective 3: Define proof.

[11.6.3.45] *Dynamic Item*

45. Which choice gives an example that supports the conjecture, and a counterexample that shows the conjecture is false?
     The multiples of 8 are divisible by 16.

   [A] $8 \times 4 = 32$ is divisible by 16, but $8 \times 3 = 24$ is not.

   [B] $8 \times 3 = 24$ is divisible by 16, but $8 \times 4 = 32$ is not.

   [C] $8 \times 4 = 32$ is divisible by 16, but $8 \times 6 = 48$ is not.

   [D] $8 \times 5 = 40$ is divisible by 16, but $8 \times 3 = 24$ is not.

[11.6.3.46] *Dynamic Item*

46. Which term is defined as "a basic statement which is accepted as true without proof?"

   [A] conjecture   [B] axiom   [C] theorem   [D] converse

[11.6.3.47] *Dynamic Item*

47. Determine whether the statement $x - 1 = x + 1$ is sometimes true, always true, never true or whether there is not enough information to tell.

[11.6.3.48] *Dynamic Item*

48. Is the following an example of inductive or deductive reasoning?
     The last 10 times you pushed an odd–numbered button a red light flashed. Therefore, if you push the button numbered 5, a red light will flash.

Lesson 6: Proof in Algebra

Objective 4: Prove theorems stated in conditional form.

[11.6.4.49] *Dynamic Item*

49. Complete the missing step of the following proof:
     If $-4x - 9 = -6x + 7$, then $x = 8$

Conclusions	Justifications
$-4x - 9 = -6x + 7$	Given
$-9 = -2x + 7$	Addition Property of Equality
$-16 = -2x$	Subtraction Property of Equality
$8 = x$	Division Property of Equality
?	?

   [A] $x = 8$; Symmetric Property of Equality

   [B] $x = 8$; Transitive Property of Equality

   [C] $x = 8$; Reflexive Property of Equality   [D] $x = 8$; Distributive Property

[11.6.4.50] *Dynamic Item*

50. Which property is shown by the following statement?
     $7 \times 1 = 7$

   [A] Identity Property ($\times$)   [B] Associative Property ($\times$)

   [C] Associative Property ($+$)   [D] Distributive Property

[11.6.4.51] *Dynamic Item*

51. Write a two-column proof of at least five steps:
     Given: $14x - 5 = -15x + 3$

     Prove: $x = \dfrac{8}{29}$

Lesson 6: Proof in Algebra

[11.6.4.52] *Dynamic Item*

52. Find three odd integers whose sum is 69 or provide a counterexample to show it is impossible.

Lesson 1: Inverse Variation

Objective 1: Define and use two different forms of inverse variation to study real-world situations.

[11.1.1.1] *Dynamic Item*

[1] [B]

[11.1.1.2] *Dynamic Item*

[2] [B]

[11.1.1.3] *Dynamic Item*

[3] $15.48

[11.1.1.4] *Dynamic Item*

[4] $4\dfrac{4}{5}$ hr

Lesson 2: Rational Expressions and Functions

Objective 1: Define and illustrate the use of rational expressions and functions.

[11.2.1.5] *Dynamic Item*

[5] [D]

[11.2.1.6] *Dynamic Item*

[6] [B]

[11.2.1.7] *Dynamic Item*

[7] $y = \dfrac{5}{x} - 1$

[11.2.1.8] *Dynamic Item*

[8] $-\dfrac{1}{12}$ and undefined

Lesson 3: Simplifying Rational Expressions

Objective 1: Factor the numerator and denominator to simplify rational expressions.

[11.3.1.9] *Dynamic Item*

[9] [C]

[11.3.1.10] *Dynamic Item*

[10] [B]

[11.3.1.11] *Dynamic Item*

[11] $\dfrac{1}{-x-8}$, $x \neq 7$, and $x \neq -8$

[11.3.1.12] *Dynamic Item*

[12] $\dfrac{x-2}{x-10}$, $x \neq 10$, $x \neq 3$

Objective 2: State the restrictions on the variable of a simplified rational expression.

[11.3.2.13] *Dynamic Item*

[13] [C]

[11.3.2.14] *Dynamic Item*

[14] [A]

[11.3.2.15] *Dynamic Item*

[15] The expression is undefined at $j = -9$, $j = 0$, and $j = 2$.

[11.3.2.16] *Dynamic Item*

[16] $p = 4$ and $p = 2$

Objective 3: Extend simplification techniques to other algebraic fractions.

[11.3.3.17] *Dynamic Item*

[17] [B]

[11.3.3.18] *Dynamic Item*

[18] [C]

[11.3.3.19] *Dynamic Item*

[19] $\dfrac{2 + e}{3}$

[11.3.3.20] *Dynamic Item*

[20] $\dfrac{a}{8b}$

Lesson 4: Operations With Rational Expressions

Objective 1: Perform operations with rational expressions in a real-world example.

[11.4.1.21] *Dynamic Item*

[21] [A]

[11.4.1.22] *Dynamic Item*

[22] [B]

[11.4.1.23] *Dynamic Item*

[23] 48 pt

[11.4.1.24] *Dynamic Item*

$$\frac{6.25x + 350}{x}$$

When $x = 100$, $A = \$9.75$. When $x = 1000$, $A = \$6.60$. When $x = 10,000$, $A = \$6.29$. As
[24] production level increases, the average cost of producing each t-shirt decreases.

Objective 2: Add, subtract, multiply, and divide rational expressions.

[11.4.2.25] *Dynamic Item*

[25] [D]

[11.4.2.26] *Dynamic Item*

[26] [C]

[11.4.2.27] *Dynamic Item*

[27] $\dfrac{n}{5}$; $n \neq 4$; $n \neq -4$

[11.4.2.28] *Dynamic Item*

[28] $\dfrac{1}{7-x}$; $x \neq \pm 7$

Lesson 5: Solving Rational Equations

Objective 1: Solve rational equations by using the common-denominator method.

[11.5.1.29] *Dynamic Item*

[29] [B]

[11.5.1.30] *Dynamic Item*

[30] [C]

[11.5.1.31] *Dynamic Item*

[31] $x = -3$

[11.5.1.32] *Dynamic Item*

[32] no solution

Objective 2: Solve rational equations by graphing.

[11.5.2.33] *Dynamic Item*

[33] [A]

[11.5.2.34] *Dynamic Item*

[34] [B]

[11.5.2.35] *Dynamic Item*

[35]   no solution

[11.5.2.36] *Dynamic Item*

[36] $x = 3$

Lesson 6: Proof in Algebra

Objective 1: Define the parts of a conditional statement.

[11.6.1.37] *Dynamic Item*

[37] [B]

[11.6.1.38] *Dynamic Item*

[38] [B]

[11.6.1.39] *Dynamic Item*

[39]   Hypothesis: The last digit of a number is 0.
Conclusion: The number is divisible by 2.

[11.6.1.40] *Dynamic Item*

[40]   Hypothesis: $8x < 24$
Conclusion: $x < 3$

Objective 2: Define converse.

[11.6.2.41] *Dynamic Item*

[41] [D]

[11.6.2.42] *Dynamic Item*

[42] [B]

[11.6.2.43] *Dynamic Item*

[43] If the sum of the digits of a number is divisible by 9, then the number is divisible by 9.

[11.6.2.44] *Dynamic Item*

[44] true; if n is odd, then n^2 is odd; true

Objective 3: Define proof.

[11.6.3.45] *Dynamic Item*

[45] [A]

[11.6.3.46] *Dynamic Item*

[46] [B]

[11.6.3.47] *Dynamic Item*

[47] never true

[11.6.3.48] *Dynamic Item*

[48] inductive

Objective 4: Prove theorems stated in conditional form.

[11.6.4.49] *Dynamic Item*

[49] [A]

[11.6.4.50] *Dynamic Item*

[50] [A]

[11.6.4.51] *Dynamic Item*

Statements	Reasons
$14x - 5 = -15x + 3$	Given
$-5 = -29x + 3$	Subtraction Property of Equality
$-8 = -29x$	Subtraction Property of Equality
$\dfrac{8}{29} = x$	Division Property of Equality
$x = \dfrac{8}{29}$	Symmetric Property of Equality

[51]

[11.6.4.52] *Dynamic Item*

[52] Answers will vary. One possible answer is $21 + 23 + 25$.

Lesson 1: Operations with Radicals

Objective 1: Identify or estimate square roots.

[12.1.1.1] *Dynamic Item*

1. Find the square root. If the square root is irrational, approximate the value to the nearest hundredth.

$\sqrt{49}$

[A] 0.7   [B] 70   [C] 7   [D] 49

[12.1.1.2] *Dynamic Item*

2. Find the square root. If the square root is irrational, approximate the value to the nearest hundredth.

$\sqrt{\dfrac{9}{16}}$

[A] $\dfrac{5}{6}$ [B] $\dfrac{3}{8}$ [C] $\dfrac{3}{4}$ [D] $\dfrac{3}{16}$

[12.1.1.3] *Dynamic Item*

3. Find the square root. If the square root is irrational, approximate the value to the nearest hundredth.

$\sqrt{21}$

[12.1.1.4] *Dynamic Item*

4. Find the square root. If the square root is irrational, approximate the value to the nearest hundredth.

$\sqrt{1.96}$

Lesson 1: Operations with Radicals

Objective 2: Define and write square roots in simplest radical form.

[12.1.2.5] *Dynamic Item*

5. Express in simplest radical form.   [A] $5\sqrt{10}$ [B] $2\sqrt{5}$ [C] $5\sqrt{2}$ [D] $10\sqrt{5}$
$\sqrt{50}$

[12.1.2.6] *Dynamic Item*

6. Express in simplest radical form.
$\sqrt{36x^5y^8}$

   [A] $6x^2y^4\sqrt{x}$ [B] $\sqrt{36x^5y^8}$ [C] $6\sqrt{x^5y^8}$ [D] $\sqrt{x}$

[12.1.2.7] *Dynamic Item*

7. Express in simplest radical form.
$\sqrt{\dfrac{7}{2}}$

[12.1.2.8] *Dynamic Item*

8. Express in simplest radical form.
$\sqrt{\dfrac{x^{10}}{y^6}}$

Lesson 1: Operations with Radicals

Objective 3: Perform mathematical operations with radicals.

[12.1.3.9] *Dynamic Item*

9. Perform the indicated operation and simplify your answer.
   $\sqrt{11} \cdot \sqrt{55}$

   [A] 11   [B] $11\sqrt{5}$ [C] 605   [D] $121\sqrt{5}$

[12.1.3.10] *Dynamic Item*

10. Perform the indicated operations and simplify your answer.
    $\left(7 - \sqrt{3}\right)\left(7 + \sqrt{3}\right)$

    [A] $46 - 14\sqrt{3}$ [B] $52 - 14\sqrt{3}$ [C] 46   [D] 52

[12.1.3.11] *Dynamic Item*

11. Perform the indicated operations and simplify your answer.
    $$\frac{\sqrt{10} + \sqrt{110}}{\sqrt{10}}$$

[12.1.3.12] *Dynamic Item*

12. Perform the indicated operations and simplify your answer.
    $6\sqrt{6} + 5\sqrt{6} - 5\sqrt{6}$

Lesson 2: Square-Root Functions and Radical Equations

Objective 1: Solve equations containing radicals.

[12.2.1.13] *Dynamic Item*

13. The motion of the leg of a robot can be modeled by the equation for a pendulum,

$t = 2\pi\sqrt{\dfrac{l}{32}}$, where l is the length of the pendulum in feet, or the robot's leg, and t is the

number of seconds required for one complete swing. Determine the length of the robot's leg if the time required for one swing is 1.8 seconds.

[A] 2.93 ft   [B] 2.63 ft   [C] 3.24 ft   [D] 2.34 ft

[12.2.1.14] *Dynamic Item*

14. Solve the equation algebraically. Be sure to check your solution(s).
$\sqrt{x+12} = x$

[A] −3   [B] 4, −3   [C] 4   [D] no solution

[12.2.1.15] *Dynamic Item*

15. Solve the equation algebraically. Be sure to check your solution(s).
$\sqrt{2x-6} = 4$

[12.2.1.16] *Dynamic Item*

16. Solve the equation algebraically. Be sure to check your solution(s).
$\sqrt{x+7} = x+5$

Objective 2: Solve equations by using radicals.

[12.2.2.17] *Dynamic Item*

17. Solve: $16x^2 = 81$ [A] $-\dfrac{9}{4}, \dfrac{9}{4}$ [B] $-\dfrac{4}{9}, \dfrac{4}{9}$ [C] $-\dfrac{81}{16}, \dfrac{81}{16}$ [D] $-\dfrac{16}{81}, \dfrac{16}{81}$

Lesson 2: Square-Root Functions and Radical Equations

[12.2.2.18] *Dynamic Item*

18. Solve: $4x^2 - 8x + 4 = 1$ [A] $-\dfrac{1}{2}, \dfrac{3}{2}$ [B] $\dfrac{1}{2}, \dfrac{3}{2}$ [C] $\dfrac{1}{2}, -\dfrac{3}{2}$ [D] $-\dfrac{1}{2}, -\dfrac{3}{2}$

[12.2.2.19] *Dynamic Item*

19. Solve: $x^2 = 20$

[12.2.2.20] *Dynamic Item*

20. The formula for kinetic energy is $E = \dfrac{1}{2}mv^2$, where E is the kinetic energy in joules,

     m is the mass of the object in kilograms, and v is the velocity of the object in meters per second. A child having a mass of 40.0 kilograms is on a sled having a mass of 7.0 kilograms. If the child and sled traveling together have a kinetic energy of 240 joules, how fast are they moving?

Lesson 3: The Pythagorean Theorem

Objective 1: Find a side length of a right triangle given the lengths of its other two sides.

[12.3.1.21] *Dynamic Item*

21. An equilateral triangle has a side length of 18 cm. Which is the altitude of the triangle?

     [A] $18\sqrt{3}$ cm   [B] 18 cm   [C] $9\sqrt{3}$ cm   [D] 36 cm

Lesson 3: The Pythagorean Theorem

[12.3.1.22] *Dynamic Item*

22. The lengths of the sides of four triangles are given. Determine which triangle is *not* a right triangle.

    [A] 10 mm, 24 mm, 26 mm   [B] 20 mm, 48 mm, 52 mm

    [C] 5 mm, 12 mm, 13 mm   [D] 11 mm, 24 mm, 26 mm

[12.3.1.23] *Dynamic Item*

23. A rectangle has a length of 11 inches and a width of 6 inches. Find the length of its diagonal to the nearest hundredth.

[12.3.1.24] *Dynamic Item*

24. Find the length of the missing side.

Lesson 3: The Pythagorean Theorem

Objective 2: Apply the Pythagorean Theorem to real-world problems.

[12.3.2.25] *Dynamic Item*

25. The city commission wants to construct a new street that connects Main Street and North Boulevard as shown in the diagram below. The construction cost has been estimated at $120 per linear foot. If there are 5280 feet in 1 mile, find the estimated cost for constructing the street. Main Street is perpendicular to North Boulevard.

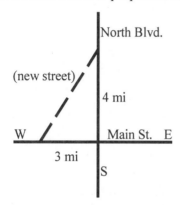

[A] $633,600   [B] $26,400   [C] $600   [D] $3,168,000

[12.3.2.26] *Dynamic Item*

26. Mr. Jones built a fenced-in area for his horse in the shape of a square with each side 35 feet in length. Find the distance of the diagonal path from one corner to the opposite corner.

[A] 2,450 ft   [B] 140 ft   [C] $35\sqrt{2}$ ft   [D] 1,225 ft

Lesson 3: The Pythagorean Theorem

[12.3.2.27] *Dynamic Item*

27. Find the altitude of the pyramid.

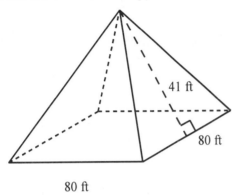

[12.3.2.28] *Dynamic Item*

28. To avoid a large, shallow reef, a ship set a course from point A and traveled 20 miles east to point B. The ship then turned and traveled 20 miles south to point C. If the ship could have traveled in a straight line from point A to point C, what is the distance the ship would have traveled? Round your answer to the nearest whole mile.

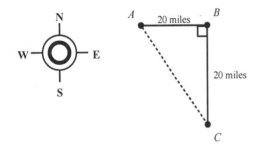

Lesson 4: The Distance Formula

Objective 1: Use the distance formula to find the distance between two points in a coordinate plane.

[12.4.1.29] *Dynamic Item*

29. Which is the length of the hypotenuse of the triangle?

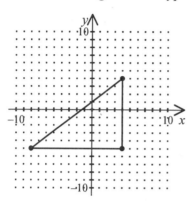

[A] 12.04   [B] 15   [C] 4.12   [D] 9.85

[12.4.1.30] *Dynamic Item*

30. Find the distance between the pair of points $(-13, 3)$ and $(-7, 19)$.

[A] 17.09   [B] 30.53   [C] 27.86   [D] 29.73

[12.4.1.31] *Dynamic Item*

31. Verify that the triangle with vertices $B(-7, 0)$, $C(-1, 0)$, and $D(-4, -4)$ is an isosceles triangle.

[12.4.1.32] *Dynamic Item*

32. Quadrilateral $ABCD$ has vertices $A(3, 2)$, $B(8, 2)$, $C(10, 6)$, and $D(5, 6)$. Find the length of each side of the quadrilateral. Leave answers in simplified radical form, if necessary.

Lesson 4: The Distance Formula

Objective 2: Determine whether a triangle is a right triangle.

[12.4.2.33] *Dynamic Item*

33. Two vertices of a triangle are $A(-2, 0)$ and $B(-13, 0)$. Which coordinates for C would make $\triangle ABC$ a right triangle?

   [A] $(-11, -2)$ [B] $(-2, 1)$ [C] $(-11, 1)$ [D] $(1, -13)$

[12.4.2.34] *Dynamic Item*

34. Given two points $R(-10, 3)$ and $S(9, 6)$, which of the following points will form right triangle *RST*?

   [A] $T(-6, -15)$ [B] $T(-7, 22)$ [C] $T(-29, 0)$ [D] $T(-7, -16)$

[12.4.2.35] *Dynamic Item*

35. Determine whether the triangle in the graph is a right triangle. Explain.

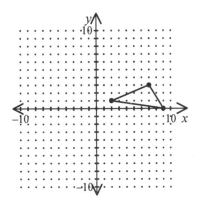

[12.4.2.36] *Dynamic Item*

36. Verify that the triangle with vertices $T(-8, 1)$, $U(0, 7)$, and $V(-4, -1)$ is a right triangle.

Lesson 4: The Distance Formula

Objective 3: Apply the midpoint formula.

[12.4.3.37] *Dynamic Item*

37. The midsegment of a trapezoid connects the midpoints of the two non-parallel sides. Find the midpoint of the midsegment of the trapezoid if $A = (4e, 4f)$, $B = (4g, 4f)$, and $C = (4h, 0)$.

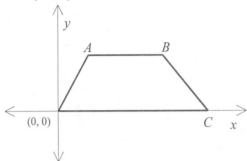

[A] $(2e + 2g, 2f + 2f)$ [B] $(g + 2h, 2f)$

[C] $(f + g + h, f)$ [D] $(e + g + h, 2f)$

[12.4.3.38] *Dynamic Item*

38. Which are the coordinates of the midpoint of the segment connecting $(-11, -7)$ and $(-4, -18)$?

[A] $(15, 25)$ [B] $\left(-\dfrac{7}{2}, \dfrac{11}{2}\right)$ [C] $(-15, -25)$ [D] $\left(-\dfrac{15}{2}, -\dfrac{25}{2}\right)$

[12.4.3.39] *Dynamic Item*

39. $M(-2, 4)$ is the midpoint of $\overline{RS}$. If S has coordinates $(5, 7)$, find the coordinates of R.

[12.4.3.40] *Dynamic Item*

40. The center of a circle is $C(-3, -3)$. One endpoint of a diameter is $D(-2, -6)$. Find the other endpoint.

Algebra 1

Lesson 5: Geometric Properties

Objective 1: Define and use the equation of a circle.

[12.5.1.41] *Dynamic Item*

41. From the equation of a circle $(x-3)^2 + (y-6)^2 = 144$, which are the center and radius?

   [A] (6, 3); 144   [B] (-3, -6); 12   [C] (6, -3); 12   [D] (3, 6); 12

[12.5.1.42] *Dynamic Item*

42. Which is the equation of the circle with its center at the origin and radius 5?

   [A] $x^2 + y^2 = 10$ [B] $x^2 + y^2 = 25$ [C] $x^2 + y^2 = 5$ [D] $\dfrac{x^2}{10} + \dfrac{x^2}{10} = 1$

[12.5.1.43] *Dynamic Item*

43. Write an equation for the circle shown in the graph.

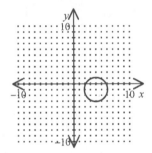

[12.5.1.44] *Dynamic Item*

44. Find the equation of the circle with center (-1, 4) and a radius of 4.

Lesson 5: Geometric Properties

Objective 2: Use the coordinate plane to investigate the diagonals of a rectangle and the midsegment of a triangle.

[12.5.2.45] *Dynamic Item*

45. Given triangle PQR with vertices $P(10, -2)$, $Q(-4, 9)$ and $R(-10, 1)$, find the length of the midsegment connecting the midpoint of $\overline{PQ}$ to the midpoint of $\overline{PR}$.

   [A] 5   [B] $\sqrt{317}$ [C] 10   [D] $\sqrt{409}$

[12.5.2.46] *Dynamic Item*

46. Given triangle RCS with vertices $R(3, 4)$, $C(-3, 2)$ and $S(-5, -5)$, find the slope of the midsegment connecting $\overline{RC}$ and $\overline{RS}$.

   [A] $\dfrac{2}{7}$ [B] $\dfrac{7}{2}$ [C] $-\dfrac{7}{2}$ [D] $-\dfrac{2}{7}$

[12.5.2.47] *Dynamic Item*

47. Given triangle PQR with vertices $P(-2, -2)$, $Q(4, -1)$ and $R(8, -11)$, find the length of the midsegment $\overline{NM}$ connecting the midpoint of $\overline{PQ}$ to the midpoint of $\overline{PR}$. Find the slope of $\overline{QR}$ and $\overline{NM}$.

[12.5.2.48] *Dynamic Item*

48. A rectangle has its vertices at $A(4, 0)$, $B(3, 0)$, $C(3, -13)$, and $D(4, -13)$. Find the lengths of the two diagonals, $\overline{AC}$ and $\overline{BD}$, and their point of intersection.

Lesson 6: The Tangent Function

Objective 1: Identify and use the tangent ratio in a right triangle.

[12.6.1.49] *Dynamic Item*

49. Find $\tan A$ for the right triangle below:

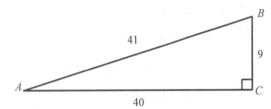

[A] $\dfrac{40}{9}$　　　　[B] $\dfrac{40}{41}$　　　　[C] $\dfrac{9}{40}$　　　　[D] $\dfrac{9}{41}$

[12.6.1.50] *Dynamic Item*

50. Use a calculator to find the measure of angle C if $\tan C = 0.0524$.

　[A] 87°　　　　[B] 57°　　　　[C] 3°　　　　[D] 42°

[12.6.1.51] *Dynamic Item*

51. Find the value of $\tan 44°$.

[12.6.1.52] *Dynamic Item*

52. Define $\tan B$.

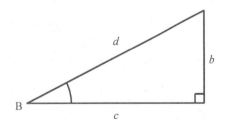

Lesson 6: The Tangent Function

Objective 2: Find unknown side and angle measures in right triangles.

[12.6.2.53] *Dynamic Item*

53. Solve for *x*. Round answers to the nearest tenth.

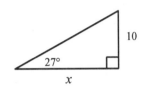

[A] 5.1   [B] 11.2   [C] 19.6   [D] 22.0

[12.6.2.54] *Dynamic Item*

54. A ladder leans against a building, forming an angle of 57° with the ground. The base of the ladder is 5 feet from the building, as seen in the diagram below. At what height does the ladder touch the building?

[A] 9.18 ft   [B] 7.70 ft   [C] 7.30 ft   [D] 5.96 ft

[12.6.2.55] *Dynamic Item*

55. A ranger spots a forest fire while on a 30 meter observation tower. The angle of depression from the tower to the fire is 13°. To the nearest meter, how far is the fire from the base of the tower?

Lesson 6: The Tangent Function

[12.6.2.56] *Dynamic Item*

56. For the triangle, find the measure of the marked acute angle to the nearest degree.

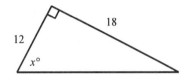

Lesson 7: The Sine and Cosine Functions

Objective 1: Define the sine and cosine ratios in a right triangle.

[12.7.1.57] *Dynamic Item*

57. Which is the value of sin 12°?

[A] 0.2079   [B] 0.2126   [C] −0.0221   [D] 0.9781

[12.7.1.58] *Dynamic Item*

58. Which is the value of cos x?

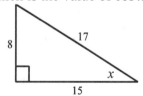

[A] $\dfrac{15}{17}$ [B] $\dfrac{8}{17}$ [C] $\dfrac{8}{15}$ [D] $\dfrac{15}{8}$

[12.7.1.59] *Dynamic Item*

59. Find the measure of $\angle P$ whose sine is 0.4848.

Lesson 7: The Sine and Cosine Functions

[12.7.1.60] *Dynamic Item*

60. In the right triangle below, $\dfrac{8}{17}$ is the value of which two trigonometric expressions?

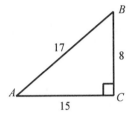

Objective 2: Find unknown side and angle measures in right triangles.

[12.7.2.61] *Dynamic Item*

61. A ladder leans against a building, forming an angle of 55° with the ground. The base of the ladder is 7 feet from the building, as seen in the diagram below. To the nearest hundredth of a foot, how long is the ladder?

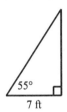

[A] 11.88 ft   [B] 8.55 ft   [C] 10.00 ft   [D] 12.20 ft

Lesson 7: The Sine and Cosine Functions

[12.7.2.62] *Dynamic Item*

62. Given that $m\angle A = 34°$ and $a = 18$, find c in the right triangle below. Round your answer to the nearest tenth.

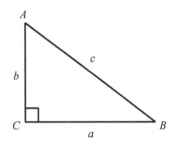

[A] 32.2   [B] 21.7   [C] 14.9   [D] 34.0

[12.7.2.63] *Dynamic Item*

63. Find the value of x to the nearest degree.

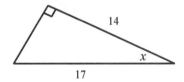

[12.7.2.64] *Dynamic Item*

64. A slide 3.1 meters long makes an angle of 33° with the ground. How high is the top of the slide above the ground?

Lesson 8: Introduction to Matrices

Objective 1: Determine the dimensions and addresses of a matrix.

[12.8.1.65] *Dynamic Item*

65. Which is the entry at the address a_{31}?   [A] 7   [B] –26   [C] –4   [D] 31

$$\begin{bmatrix} 29 & -27 & -4 & -16 \\ 16 & 18 & -26 & -17 \\ 7 & 25 & -9 & -10 \end{bmatrix}$$

[12.8.1.66] *Dynamic Item*

66. A supermarket chain sells oranges, apples, peaches, and bananas in three stores located throughout a large metropolitan area. The average number of pounds sold per day in each store is summarized in matrix M. Which is the entry at address m_{34}?

Fruit

	Oranges	Apples	Peaches	Bananas	
	50	55	45	50	Store 1
$M =$	35	70	50	80	Store 2
	70	50	60	55	Store 3

[A] 80   [B] 50   [C] 55   [D] 60

Lesson 8: Introduction to Matrices

[12.8.1.67] *Dynamic Item*

67. Find the dimensions of the matrix.

$$\begin{bmatrix} 3 & 5 & 6 & 4 & 8 & 9 & 5 & 6 & 4 & 1 \\ 9 & 1 & 8 & 9 & 1 & 4 & 6 & 7 & 2 & 2 \\ 6 & 7 & 5 & 6 & 7 & 8 & 1 & 3 & 3 & 9 \\ 8 & 1 & 2 & 7 & 9 & 0 & 2 & 0 & 9 & 3 \\ 0 & 9 & 1 & 3 & 5 & 3 & 9 & 6 & 1 & 4 \\ 4 & 3 & 8 & 5 & 0 & 1 & 4 & 7 & 5 & 6 \\ 7 & 4 & 0 & 2 & 4 & 2 & 5 & 8 & 8 & 7 \\ 2 & 0 & 2 & 6 & 3 & 7 & 8 & 0 & 5 & 0 \end{bmatrix}$$

[12.8.1.68] *Dynamic Item*

68. Write a 2×3 matrix which could represent different prices for child, adult, and senior tickets at a movie theater for matinee and evening shows.

Objective 2: Determine whether two matrices are equal.

[12.8.2.69] *Dynamic Item*

69. Find the values of the variables.

$$\begin{bmatrix} -4 & 7t+6 \\ -3 & 6 \end{bmatrix} = \begin{bmatrix} -4 & 5t-3 \\ -3 & 2y-2 \end{bmatrix}$$

[A] $t = -\dfrac{9}{2}; \ y = -1$ [B] $t = -5; \ y = 4$ [C] $t = -\dfrac{9}{2}; \ y = 4$ [D] $t = -5; \ y = -1$

Lesson 8: Introduction to Matrices

[12.8.2.70] *Dynamic Item*

70. Which of the following matrices is equal to matrix A?

$$A = \begin{bmatrix} -6+3 & 5-8 \\ 2^2 & \sqrt{4} \\ -\dfrac{10}{6} & 44-18 \end{bmatrix}$$

[A] $\begin{bmatrix} -3 & -2 \\ 4 & 3 \\ \dfrac{5}{3} & 26 \end{bmatrix}$
[B] $\begin{bmatrix} -3 & -3 \\ 4 & 2 \\ -\dfrac{5}{3} & 26 \end{bmatrix}$
[C] $\begin{bmatrix} -3 & -3 \\ 4 & 3 \\ -\dfrac{5}{3} & 26 \end{bmatrix}$
[D] $\begin{bmatrix} -3 & -2 \\ 4 & 2 \\ \dfrac{5}{3} & 26 \end{bmatrix}$

[12.8.2.71] *Dynamic Item*

71. Find the values of the variables.

$$\begin{bmatrix} 5x-7 & -5 \\ -9 & 6m-3 \end{bmatrix} = \begin{bmatrix} -7 & -5 \\ -9 & 8m+2 \end{bmatrix}$$

[12.8.2.72] *Dynamic Item*

72. Is matrix A equal to matrix B? If not, explain.

$$A = \begin{bmatrix} 12(2) & 4^2 & 4-1 \\ 3-3 & 120 \div 4 & 3(4) \end{bmatrix} \qquad B = \begin{bmatrix} 3(8) & 19-3 & 2+1 \\ 0 & 6(5) & 3+8 \end{bmatrix}$$

Lesson 8: Introduction to Matrices

Objective 3: Add, subtract, and multiply matrices.

[12.8.3.73] *Dynamic Item*

73. Perform the indicated matrix operation.

$$\begin{bmatrix} 6 & -6 & 7 \\ 8 & -2 & 0 \\ 9 & -9 & 3 \end{bmatrix} + \begin{bmatrix} 4 & -5 & -8 \\ 0 & 2 & -6 \\ -4 & 6 & -1 \end{bmatrix}$$

[A] $\begin{bmatrix} 2 & -1 & 15 \\ 8 & -4 & 4 \\ 13 & -15 & 6 \end{bmatrix}$
[B] $\begin{bmatrix} 2 & -1 & 15 \\ 8 & -4 & 6 \\ 13 & -15 & 4 \end{bmatrix}$

[C] $\begin{bmatrix} 10 & -11 & -1 \\ 8 & 0 & 2 \\ 5 & -3 & -6 \end{bmatrix}$
[D] $\begin{bmatrix} 10 & -11 & -1 \\ 8 & 0 & -6 \\ 5 & -3 & 2 \end{bmatrix}$

[12.8.3.74] *Dynamic Item*

74. Perform the indicated matrix operation.

$$\begin{bmatrix} 0 & -2 & 1 \\ -1 & -1 & 0 \end{bmatrix} \begin{bmatrix} 1 & 6 \\ 0 & 1 \\ 1 & -1 \end{bmatrix}$$

[A] $\begin{bmatrix} 1 & -3 \\ -1 & -7 \end{bmatrix}$
[B] $\begin{bmatrix} 1 & -1 \\ -3 & -7 \end{bmatrix}$
[C] $\begin{bmatrix} -6 & -8 & 1 \\ -1 & -1 & 0 \\ 1 & -1 & 0 \end{bmatrix}$
[D] $\begin{bmatrix} 0 & -6 \\ 0 & -1 \\ 0 & 0 \end{bmatrix}$

[12.8.3.75] *Dynamic Item*

75. Perform the indicated matrix operation.

$$-2 \begin{bmatrix} 5 & -1 & 2 \\ 8 & 6 & 7 \\ 0 & -9 & -6 \end{bmatrix}$$

Lesson 8: Introduction to Matrices

[12.8.3.76] *Dynamic Item*

76. Perform the indicated matrix operation.

$$\begin{bmatrix} 6 & -2 \\ 3 & -4 \end{bmatrix}\begin{bmatrix} 5 & 4 \\ -2 & -6 \end{bmatrix}$$

Objective 4: Determine the multiplicative identity of a matrix.

[12.8.4.77] *Dynamic Item*

77. Which of the following matrices, when multiplied by matrix A, gives the identity matrix for A?

$$A = \begin{bmatrix} 1 & -5 \\ -4 & -2 \end{bmatrix}$$

[A] $\begin{bmatrix} -\dfrac{1}{22} & -\dfrac{2}{11} \\ -\dfrac{5}{22} & \dfrac{1}{11} \end{bmatrix}$ [B] $\begin{bmatrix} -2 & -4 \\ -5 & 1 \end{bmatrix}$ [C] $\begin{bmatrix} \dfrac{1}{11} & -\dfrac{5}{22} \\ -\dfrac{2}{11} & -\dfrac{1}{22} \end{bmatrix}$ [D] None of these

[12.8.4.78] *Dynamic Item*

78. If $N = \begin{bmatrix} -8 & -7 & -4 \\ -9 & 5 & -2 \\ -3 & 6 & -8 \end{bmatrix}$, which of the following is I, the identity matrix, so that $N \cdot I = N$?

[A] $\begin{bmatrix} \dfrac{1}{-8} & \dfrac{1}{-7} & \dfrac{1}{-4} \\ \dfrac{1}{-9} & \dfrac{1}{5} & \dfrac{1}{-2} \\ \dfrac{1}{-3} & \dfrac{1}{6} & \dfrac{1}{-8} \end{bmatrix}$ [B] $\begin{bmatrix} 1 & 0 & 0 \\ 0 & 1 & 0 \\ 0 & 0 & 1 \end{bmatrix}$ [C] $\begin{bmatrix} 1 & 1 & 1 \\ 1 & 1 & 1 \\ 1 & 1 & 1 \end{bmatrix}$ [D] $\begin{bmatrix} 8 & 7 & 4 \\ 9 & -5 & 2 \\ 3 & -6 & 8 \end{bmatrix}$

Lesson 8: Introduction to Matrices

[12.8.4.79] *Dynamic Item*

79. If $N = \begin{bmatrix} 7 & 6 & 5 \\ 2 & -1 & 4 \\ -3 & 9 & -8 \end{bmatrix}$, find I, the identity matrix, so that $N \cdot I = N$.

[12.8.4.80] *Dynamic Item*

80. If possible, find the identity matrix for the given matrix. If not possible, explain why not.

$\begin{bmatrix} 0 & -1 \\ 2 & 4 \end{bmatrix}$

Lesson 1: Operations with Radicals

Objective 1: Identify or estimate square roots.

[12.1.1.1] *Dynamic Item*

[1] [C]

[12.1.1.2] *Dynamic Item*

[2] [C]

[12.1.1.3] *Dynamic Item*

[3] 4.58

[12.1.1.4] *Dynamic Item*

[4] 1.4

Objective 2: Define and write square roots in simplest radical form.

[12.1.2.5] *Dynamic Item*

[5] [C]

[12.1.2.6] *Dynamic Item*

[6] [A]

[12.1.2.7] *Dynamic Item*

[7] $\dfrac{\sqrt{14}}{2}$

[12.1.2.8] *Dynamic Item*

[8] $\dfrac{|x|^5}{|y|^3}$

Objective 3: Perform mathematical operations with radicals.

[12.1.3.9] *Dynamic Item*

[9] [B]

[12.1.3.10] *Dynamic Item*

[10] [C]

[12.1.3.11] *Dynamic Item*

[11] $1 + \sqrt{11}$

[12.1.3.12] *Dynamic Item*

[12] $6\sqrt{6}$

Lesson 2: Square-Root Functions and Radical Equations

Objective 1: Solve equations containing radicals.

[12.2.1.13] *Dynamic Item*

[13] [B]

[12.2.1.14] *Dynamic Item*

[14] [C]

[12.2.1.15] *Dynamic Item*

[15] 11

[12.2.1.16] *Dynamic Item*

[16] $x = -3$

Objective 2: Solve equations by using radicals.

[12.2.2.17] *Dynamic Item*

[17] [A]

[12.2.2.18] *Dynamic Item*

[18] [B]

[12.2.2.19] *Dynamic Item*

[19] $-2\sqrt{5},\ 2\sqrt{5}$

[12.2.2.20] *Dynamic Item*

[20] $v = 3.2$ m/s

Lesson 3: The Pythagorean Theorem

Objective 1: Find a side length of a right triangle given the lengths of its other two sides.

[12.3.1.21] *Dynamic Item*

[21] [C]

[12.3.1.22] *Dynamic Item*

[22] [D]

[12.3.1.23] *Dynamic Item*

[23] $\sqrt{157} \approx 12.53$ in.

[12.3.1.24] *Dynamic Item*

[24] 24

Objective 2: Apply the Pythagorean Theorem to real-world problems.

[12.3.2.25] *Dynamic Item*

[25] [D]

[12.3.2.26] *Dynamic Item*

[26] [C]

[12.3.2.27] *Dynamic Item*

[27] 9 ft

[12.3.2.28] *Dynamic Item*

[28] 28 miles

Lesson 4: The Distance Formula

Objective 1: Use the distance formula to find the distance between two points in a coordinate plane.

[12.4.1.29] *Dynamic Item*

[29] [B]

[12.4.1.30] *Dynamic Item*

[30] [A]

[12.4.1.31] *Dynamic Item*

[31] Students must show that only two sides are equal in length.

[12.4.1.32] *Dynamic Item*

[32] $AB = 5$; $BC = 2\sqrt{5}$; $CD = 5$; $AD = 2\sqrt{5}$

Objective 2: Determine whether a triangle is a right triangle.

[12.4.2.33] *Dynamic Item*

[33] [B]

[12.4.2.34] *Dynamic Item*

[34] [D]

[12.4.2.35] *Dynamic Item*

[35] not right, $13 + 29 \neq 50$ (The sum of the squares of the lengths of the legs $\neq$ square of the length of the hypotenuse.)

[12.4.2.36] *Dynamic Item*

[36] $\sqrt{20+80} = \sqrt{100}$

Objective 3: Apply the midpoint formula.

[12.4.3.37] *Dynamic Item*

[37] [D]

[12.4.3.38] *Dynamic Item*

[38] [D]

[12.4.3.39] *Dynamic Item*

[39] $(-9, 1)$

[12.4.3.40] *Dynamic Item*

[40] $(-4, 0)$

Lesson 5: Geometric Properties

Objective 1: Define and use the equation of a circle.

[12.5.1.41] *Dynamic Item*

[41] [D]

[12.5.1.42] *Dynamic Item*

[42] [B]

[12.5.1.43] *Dynamic Item*

[43] $(x-4)^2 + (y+1)^2 = 4$

[12.5.1.44] *Dynamic Item*

[44] $(x+1)^2 + (y-4)^2 = 16$

Objective 2: Use the coordinate plane to investigate the diagonals of a rectangle and the midsegment of a triangle.

[12.5.2.45] *Dynamic Item*

[45] [A]

[12.5.2.46] *Dynamic Item*

[46] [B]

[12.5.2.47] *Dynamic Item*

[47] $\sqrt{29}$; $-\dfrac{5}{2}$

[12.5.2.48] *Dynamic Item*

[48] The diagonals are each equal to approximately 13.04 units They intersect at $(3.5, -6.5)$

Lesson 6: The Tangent Function

Objective 1: Identify and use the tangent ratio in a right triangle.

[12.6.1.49] *Dynamic Item*

[49] [C]

[12.6.1.50] *Dynamic Item*

[50] [C]

[12.6.1.51] *Dynamic Item*

[51] 0.9657

[12.6.1.52] *Dynamic Item*

[52] $\dfrac{b}{c}$

Objective 2: Find unknown side and angle measures in right triangles.

[12.6.2.53] *Dynamic Item*

[53] [C]

[12.6.2.54] *Dynamic Item*

[54] [B]

[12.6.2.55] *Dynamic Item*

[55] 130 meters

[12.6.2.56] *Dynamic Item*

[56] 56°

Lesson 7: The Sine and Cosine Functions

Objective 1: Define the sine and cosine ratios in a right triangle.

[12.7.1.57] *Dynamic Item*

[57] [A]

[12.7.1.58] *Dynamic Item*

[58] [A]

[12.7.1.59] *Dynamic Item*

[59] 29°

[12.7.1.60] *Dynamic Item*

[60] cos B or sin A

Objective 2: Find unknown side and angle measures in right triangles.

[12.7.2.61] *Dynamic Item*

[61] [D]

[12.7.2.62] *Dynamic Item*

[62] [A]

[12.7.2.63] *Dynamic Item*

[63] 35°

[12.7.2.64] *Dynamic Item*

[64] 1.69 m

Lesson 8: Introduction to Matrices

Objective 1: Determine the dimensions and addresses of a matrix.

[12.8.1.65] *Dynamic Item*

[65] [A]

[12.8.1.66] *Dynamic Item*

[66] [C]

[12.8.1.67] *Dynamic Item*

[67] 8×10

[12.8.1.68] *Dynamic Item*

[68]

One possible answer:

	Child	Adult	Senior
Matinee	$3.50	$5.50	$3.50
Evening	$5.00	$7.50	$4.50

Objective 2: Determine whether two matrices are equal.

[12.8.2.69] *Dynamic Item*

[69] [C]

[12.8.2.70] *Dynamic Item*

[70] [B]

[12.8.2.71] *Dynamic Item*

[71] $x = 0$; $m = -\dfrac{5}{2}$

[12.8.2.72] *Dynamic Item*

[72] No; $3(4) \neq 3 + 8$

Objective 3: Add, subtract, and multiply matrices.

[12.8.3.73] *Dynamic Item*

[73] [D]

[12.8.3.74] *Dynamic Item*

[74] [A]

[12.8.3.75] *Dynamic Item*

[75] $\begin{bmatrix} -10 & 2 & -4 \\ -16 & -12 & -14 \\ 0 & 18 & 12 \end{bmatrix}$

[12.8.3.76] *Dynamic Item*

[76] $\begin{bmatrix} 34 & 36 \\ 23 & 36 \end{bmatrix}$

Objective 4: Determine the multiplicative identity of a matrix.

[12.8.4.77] *Dynamic Item*

[77] [C]

Algebra 1

[12.8.4.78] *Dynamic Item*

[78] [B]

[12.8.4.79] *Dynamic Item*

[79] $\begin{bmatrix} 1 & 0 & 0 \\ 0 & 1 & 0 \\ 0 & 0 & 1 \end{bmatrix}$

[12.8.4.80] *Dynamic Item*

[80] $\begin{bmatrix} 1 & 0 \\ 0 & 1 \end{bmatrix}$

Lesson 1: Theoretical Probability

Objective 1: List or describe the sample space of an experiment.

[13.1.1.1] *Dynamic Item*

1. A spinner that has 4 sections of equal area, numbered from 1 to 4, is spun two times in succession. Which of the following is/are *not* part of the sample space?

    I. (0, 1)   II. (4, 4)   III. (2, 4)   IV. (4, 2)

    [A] I and II only   [B] II only   [C] I only   [D] All of the outcomes are possible.

[13.1.1.2] *Dynamic Item*

2. A coin is tossed. If a head appears, a spinner that can land on any of the numbers from 1 to 4 is spun. If a tail appears, the coin is tossed a second time instead of using the spinner. Which of the following is a sample space for the experiment?

    [A] $\{(T, H), (H, H), (H, 1), (H, 2), (H, 3), (H, 4)\}$

    [B] $\{(T, H), (T, T), (T, 1), (T, 2), (T, 3), (T, 4)\}$

    [C] $\{(T, H), (H, H), (T, 1), (T, 2), (T, 3), (T, 4)\}$

    [D] $\{(T, H), (T, T), (H, 1), (H, 2), (H, 3), (H, 4)\}$

[13.1.1.3] *Dynamic Item*

3. Jane is playing a card game with her friend. She will draw two cards from those pictured.

    a. List the sample space for all possible 2-card combinations Jane could make. Note that the order of the cards does not matter.
    b. What is the probability both are even cards?

Lesson 1: Theoretical Probability

[13.1.1.4] *Dynamic Item*

4. A spinner that has 4 sections of equal area, numbered from 1 to 4, is spun two times in succession. Write the sample space.

Objective 2: Find the theoretical probability of a favorable outcome.

[13.1.2.5] *Dynamic Item*

5. There are 5 red marbles, 7 white marbles, 6 blue marbles, and 9 green marbles in a bag. Suppose you select one marble at random. What is the probability of selecting a blue marble?

   [A] $\frac{3}{7}$ [B] $\frac{7}{9}$ [C] $\frac{2}{7}$ [D] $\frac{2}{9}$

[13.1.2.6] *Dynamic Item*

6. A deck of cards is numbered 1 to 33. If you draw one card at random, what is the probability that the card you draw will have 5 as a factor?

   [A] $\frac{6}{33}$ [B] $\frac{7}{33}$ [C] $\frac{1}{5}$ [D] $\frac{5}{33}$

[13.1.2.7] *Dynamic Item*

7. Suppose two number cubes are rolled. What is the probability that a sum of 6 or 8 turns up?

[13.1.2.8] *Dynamic Item*

8. Suppose you pick one of the thirteen diamond cards in a standard deck of playing cards without looking. Find the theoretical probability of picking an Ace.

A	2	3	4	5	6	7	8	9	10	J	Q	K
♦	♦	♦	♦	♦	♦	♦	♦	♦	♦	♦	♦	♦

Lesson 2: Counting the Elements of Sets

Objective 1: Find the union and intersection of sets.

[13.2.1.9] *Dynamic Item*

9. If $A = \{0, 3, 5, 8\}$, $B = \{1, 4, 6, 9\}$, and $C = \{0, 4, 5, 6\}$, find $(A \cup C) \cap B$.

   [A] $\{1, 9\}$　　　　[B] $\{0, 3, 5, 6, 8\}$　　[C] $\{4, 6\}$　　　　[D] $\{3, 8\}$

Lesson 2: Counting the Elements of Sets

[13.2.1.10] *Dynamic Item*

10. The athletic director at Georgeville Middle School surveyed some eighth grade students to find out what sports they play. Some of the results of the survey are shown in the Venn diagram. Complete the Venn diagram using the data in the table below.

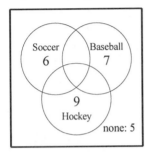

Sport	Number of Players
Soccer & Baseball	3
Soccer & Hockey	8
Hockey & Baseball	1
All three sports	4

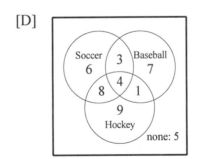

[13.2.1.11] *Dynamic Item*

11. What values of *y* make the following compound statement true?
    y is a factor of 16 or *y* is a factor of 42.

Lesson 2: Counting the Elements of Sets

[13.2.1.12] *Dynamic Item*

12. The school cafeteria asked some students whether they liked vanilla or chocolate ice cream. The results are shown in the Venn diagram below. How many students do not like vanilla ice cream?

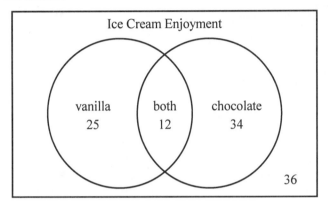

Objective 2: Count the elements of sets.

[13.2.2.13] *Dynamic Item*

13. In a standard deck of 52 playing cards, how many cards are a spade or black?

    [A] 13   [B] 28   [C] 39   [D] 26

[13.2.2.14] *Dynamic Item*

14. In a school of 449 students, 85 students are in the band, 199 students are on sports teams, and 33 students participate in both activities. How many students are involved in either band or sports?

    [A] 199   [B] 85   [C] 284   [D] 251

Lesson 2: Counting the Elements of Sets

[13.2.2.15] *Dynamic Item*

15. Southview High School is selecting a mascot for the school. Three final names have been selected. A survey is made of some students about their favorite choice. The results are shown in the table below. How many boys were in the survey?

Mascot	Bulldogs	Cougars	Buffaloes	Total
Boys	15	25	26	66
Girls	16	20	27	63
Total	31	45	53	129

[13.2.2.16] *Dynamic Item*

16. There are 41 students in the Chess Club. Twelve can only attend practice on Saturday, and 21 can only attend practice on Sunday. Five students can attend either day. How many students cannot attend at all?

Objective 3: Apply the Addition of Probabilities Principle.

[13.2.3.17] *Dynamic Item*

17. Mary has a bag that contains 3 green marbles, 8 red marbles, and 9 blue marbles. Without looking, Mary draws a marble from the bag. What is the probability that Mary will draw a red or a blue marble?

[A] $\dfrac{17}{20}$ [B] $\dfrac{1}{19}$ [C] $\dfrac{18}{95}$ [D] $\dfrac{9}{50}$

Lesson 2: Counting the Elements of Sets

[13.2.3.18] *Dynamic Item*

18. Use the Venn diagram to find the probability that a point chosen at random from the three sets is in A but not in B.

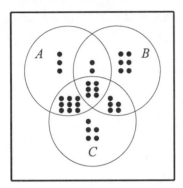

[A] $\dfrac{11}{36}$ [B] $\dfrac{1}{3}$ [C] $\dfrac{5}{36}$ [D] $\dfrac{3}{4}$

[13.2.3.19] *Dynamic Item*

19. Using the spinner below, find the probability that you spin a consonant or a capital letter.

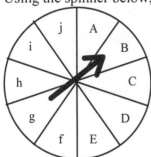

[13.2.3.20] *Dynamic Item*

20. In a deck of 52 playing cards, find the probability of drawing a card which is either a face card or a two.

Lesson 3: The Fundamental Counting Principle

Objective 1: Use tree diagrams to count the number of choices that can be made from sets.

[13.3.1.21] *Dynamic Item*

21. Which of the tree diagrams shows the various combinations for varieties of trucks if they can be blue or silver in color and be equipped with alloy wheels or non-alloy wheels?

[A]

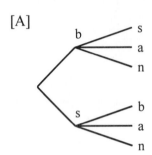

[B]

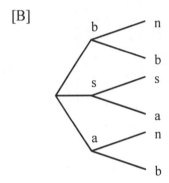

[C]

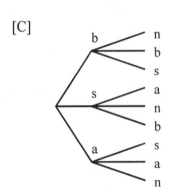

[D]

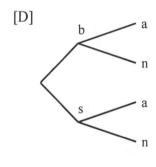

Lesson 3: The Fundamental Counting Principle

[13.3.1.22] *Dynamic Item*

22. At a pizza parlor, Isabel has a choice of pizza toppings and sizes. There are topping choices of hamburger, pepperoni, and sausage and size choices of giant and mini. Which tree diagram shows the number of possible pizza combinations that Isabel can order on a pizza, assuming only one topping is selected?

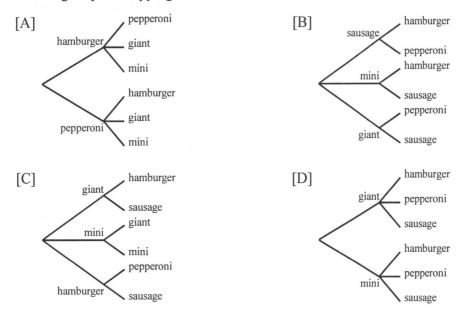

[13.3.1.23] *Dynamic Item*

23. Jeremy went to the mall to buy a shirt for a friend. His fabric choices for the shirt are wool and corduroy. Both of these choices come in blue, black and yellow. Draw a tree diagram that shows the number of shirt choices that are available to Jeremy.

[13.3.1.24] *Dynamic Item*

24. Clarissa is having lunch at a sandwich shop. Her choices for condiments are: mustard, salad dressing, or mayonnaise. Her options for fillings are: spicy tofu, egg salad, ham, or chicken. She could choose one of the following breads: rye or pumpernickel. Draw a tree diagram to show how many different sandwich choices she has, assuming she chooses one condiment, one filling, and one type of bread.

Lesson 3: The Fundamental Counting Principle

Objective 2: Use the Fundamental Counting Principle to count the number of choices that can be made from sets.

[13.3.2.25] *Dynamic Item*

25. The computer teachers at West High School decide to get vanity license plates for their cars using the letters C, O, M, P, U, T, E, and R. Use the Fundamental Counting Principle to find the number of different license plates that can be formed using all of these letters without repeating any letter.

   [A] 40,320   [B] 362,880   [C] 5040   [D] 40,340

[13.3.2.26] *Dynamic Item*

26. You and 9 friends go to a concert. Use the Fundamental Counting Principle to find how many different ways can you sit in the assigned seats?

   [A] 81   [B] 3,628,800   [C] 362,880   [D] 55

[13.3.2.27] *Dynamic Item*

27. How many different arrangements can be made using all of the letters in the word MATH?

[13.3.2.28] *Dynamic Item*

28. A lunch menu consists of 5 different kinds of sandwiches, 3 different kinds of soup, and 4 different drinks. Use the Fundamental Counting Principle to find the number of choices available for ordering a sandwich, a bowl of soup, and a drink.

Lesson 4: Independent Events

Objective 1: Find the probability of independent events.

[13.4.1.29] *Dynamic Item*

29. If the spinner is spun twice, what is the probability that the arrow will stop on a vowel both times?

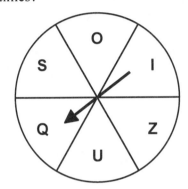

[A] $\dfrac{7}{36}$ [B] $\dfrac{1}{4}$ [C] $\dfrac{1}{3}$ [D] $\dfrac{5}{18}$

[13.4.1.30] *Dynamic Item*

30. Two bags each contain blue marbles and green marbles. The first bag contains 5 blue marbles and 3 green marbles and the second bag contains 3 blue marbles and 5 green marbles. A marble is randomly drawn from each bag. What is the probability that both marbles are blue?

[A] $\dfrac{8}{67}$ [B] $\dfrac{4}{33}$ [C] $\dfrac{3}{13}$ [D] $\dfrac{15}{64}$

Lesson 4: Independent Events

[13.4.1.31] *Dynamic Item*

31. Mr. Zadak is giving a vocabulary quiz today. There are six multiple-choice questions on the quiz, and each question has 1 correct and 3 incorrect choices.

a. What is the probability of getting a correct answer on any one question?
b. What is the probability of getting an incorrect answer on any one question?
c. Ernest didn't do his homework and knows none of the words on the quiz, so he makes a random guess on every question. What is the probability he answers all 6 questions correctly?

[13.4.1.32] *Dynamic Item*

32. Two cards are drawn with replacement from a regular deck of playing cards. Find the probability that at least one card is not a club.

Lesson 5: Simulations

Objective 1: Design and perform simulations to find experimental probabilities.

[13.5.1.33] *Dynamic Item*

33. In a box of pink and red candy, there are 4 pink candy pieces for every piece of red candy. Design a simulation to estimate the number of pieces a person must choose in order to get 4 pieces of red candy.

[A] Use a spinner with 9 sections, 5 of the sections shaded.

[B] Use a spinner with 4 sections, 3 of the sections shaded.

[C] Use a spinner with 5 sections, 4 of the sections shaded.

[D] Use a spinner with 9 sections, 4 of the sections shaded.

Lesson 5: Simulations

[13.5.1.34] *Dynamic Item*

34. Chris has made 75% of her goal kicks in soccer. How could you simulate her next 14 goal kicks?

 [A] Flip 2 coins.

 [B] Spin a spinner with 5 equal sections having 4 sections shaded.

 [C] Flip 1 coin.

 [D] Roll a die with 9 sides.

[13.5.1.35] *Dynamic Item*

35. A German professor knows that one out of every 8 people will not show up for his college class. The room has 20 chairs and the German teacher has admitted 25 students to the class. Describe a way to simulate the number of chairs that will be filled during the class period.

[13.5.1.36] *Dynamic Item*

36. Use the table of random digits below to estimate the probability that, out of 3 coin tosses, exactly 1 head occurs. Use 0 − 4 to represent heads and 5 − 9 to represent tails. The numbers have been grouped vertically to represent the 3 coins in one toss.

8 0 1 3 7 1 4 1 8 4 4 2 6 6 0 4 0 3 9 4 2 5 1 8 7 2
9 5 0 8 5 3 7 6 9 9 8 2 1 6 9 4 1 5 6 0 1 2 3 7 1 5
4 3 4 2 6 6 0 4 9 3 1 2 4 1 6 6 1 1 6 9 4 1 1 6 2 4

Lesson 1: Theoretical Probability

Objective 1: List or describe the sample space of an experiment.

[13.1.1.1] *Dynamic Item*

[1] [C]

[13.1.1.2] *Dynamic Item*

[2] [D]

[13.1.1.3] *Dynamic Item*

a. 5, 4   5, 9   5, 2   5, 8   4, 9
   4, 2   4, 8   9, 2   9, 8   2, 8

[3] b. $\dfrac{3}{10}$

[13.1.1.4] *Dynamic Item*

[4] {(1, 1), (1, 2), (1, 3), (1, 4), (2, 1), (2, 2), (2, 3), (2, 4), (3, 1), (3, 2), (3, 3), (3, 4), (4, 1), (4, 2), (4, 3), (4, 4)}

Objective 2: Find the theoretical probability of a favorable outcome.

[13.1.2.5] *Dynamic Item*

[5] [D]

[13.1.2.6] *Dynamic Item*

[6] [A]

[13.1.2.7] *Dynamic Item*

[7] $\dfrac{5}{18}$ _____

[13.1.2.8] *Dynamic Item*

[8] $\dfrac{1}{13}$ _____

Lesson 2: Counting the Elements of Sets

Objective 1: Find the union and intersection of sets.

[13.2.1.9] *Dynamic Item*

[9] [C] _____

[13.2.1.10] *Dynamic Item*

[10] [D] _____

[13.2.1.11] *Dynamic Item*

[11] 1, 2, 3, 4, 6, 7, 8, 14, 16, 21, 42 _____

[13.2.1.12] *Dynamic Item*

[12] 70 _____

Objective 2: Count the elements of sets.

[13.2.2.13] *Dynamic Item*

[13] [D] _____

[13.2.2.14] *Dynamic Item*

[14] [D]

[13.2.2.15] *Dynamic Item*

[15] 66

[13.2.2.16] *Dynamic Item*

[16] 3

Objective 3: Apply the Addition of Probabilities Principle.

[13.2.3.17] *Dynamic Item*

[17] [A]

[13.2.3.18] *Dynamic Item*

[18] [B]

[13.2.3.19] *Dynamic Item*

[19] $\dfrac{9}{10}$

[13.2.3.20] *Dynamic Item*

[20] $\dfrac{4}{13}$

Lesson 3: The Fundamental Counting Principle

Objective 1: Use tree diagrams to count the number of choices that can be made from sets.

[13.3.1.21] *Dynamic Item*

[21] [D]

[13.3.1.22] *Dynamic Item*

[22] [D]

[13.3.1.23] *Dynamic Item*

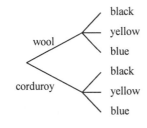

[23] _____

[13.3.1.24] *Dynamic Item*

24 choices; Student drawings may vary. One branch of a tree is given below.

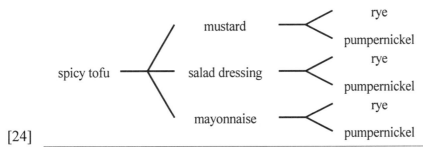

[24] _____

Objective 2: Use the Fundamental Counting Principle to count the number of choices that can be made from sets.

[13.3.2.25] *Dynamic Item*

[25] [A]

[13.3.2.26] *Dynamic Item*

[26] [B]

[13.3.2.27] *Dynamic Item*

[27] 24

[13.3.2.28] *Dynamic Item*

[28] 60

Lesson 4: Independent Events

Objective 1: Find the probability of independent events.

[13.4.1.29] *Dynamic Item*

[29] [B]

[13.4.1.30] *Dynamic Item*

[30] [D]

[13.4.1.31] *Dynamic Item*

    a. $\dfrac{1}{4}$

    b. $\dfrac{3}{4}$

[31]   c. $\dfrac{1}{4096}$

[13.4.1.32] *Dynamic Item*

[32] $\dfrac{15}{16}$

Lesson 5: Simulations

Objective 1: Design and perform simulations to find experimental probabilities.

[13.5.1.33] *Dynamic Item*

[33] [C]

[13.5.1.34] *Dynamic Item*

[34] [A]

[13.5.1.35] *Dynamic Item*

Sample answer: Use a calculator to generate numbers from 1 to 25. Use the command INT(RAND*25)+1. Decide in advance which numbers will represent students who do not
[35] show up to class. For example, all the multiples of 8.

[13.5.1.36] *Dynamic Item*

[36] $\dfrac{3}{26}$

Lesson 1: Graphing Functions and Relations

Objective 1: Use models to understand functions and relations.

[14.1.1.1] *Dynamic Item*

1. Which of the following is a model of the relation $\{(-7,-1),(-6,-1),(3,-1),(6,-1)\}$?
    Determine whether the relation is a function.

[A]

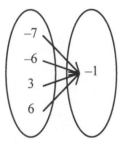

It is not a function.

[B]

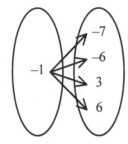

It is not a function.

[C]

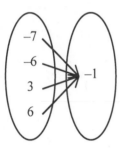

It is a function.

[D]

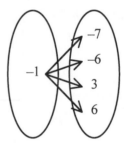

It is a function.

Lesson 1: Graphing Functions and Relations

[14.1.1.2] *Dynamic Item*

2. Determine which of the following graphs does *not* represent a function.

[A]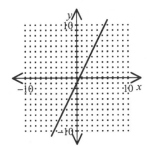

[B]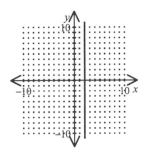

[C]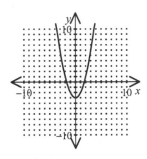

[D]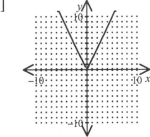

[14.1.1.3] *Dynamic Item*

3. Write the relation shown in the model in set notation. Determine whether the relation is a function.

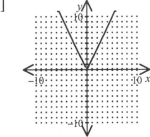

Lesson 1: Graphing Functions and Relations

[14.1.1.4] *Dynamic Item*

4. Find the domain and range of the function: $\{(5,\ 25),\ (6,\ 36),\ (7,\ 49),\ (8,\ 64)\}$

Objective 2: Evaluate functions by using function rules.

[14.1.2.5] *Dynamic Item*

5. For $f(x) = -2x^2 - 3x + 3$, evaluate $f(-3)$.   [A] –9   [B] –42   [C] 18   [D] –6

[14.1.2.6] *Dynamic Item*

6. Given $f(x) = 2x - 4$, which is an ordered pair, $(x,\ y)$ for the element in the domain $x = -3$?

   [A] $(-3,\ -10)$ [B] $(-3,\ 14)$ [C] $(-3,\ -2)$ [D] $(-3,\ -6)$

[14.1.2.7] *Dynamic Item*

7. Given the function $f(x) = -|x+4|$, give the domain and range for the function.

[14.1.2.8] *Dynamic Item*

8. For $f(x) = 3x^2$, evaluate $f(3)$.

Lesson 1: Graphing Functions and Relations

Objective 3: Identify the parent functions of some important families of functions.

[14.1.3.9] *Dynamic Item*

9. Which is the parent function for the graph shown?

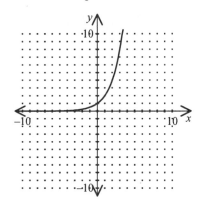

[A] $y = \dfrac{1}{x}$ [B] $y = x^2$ [C] $y = 2^x$ [D] $y = \sqrt{x}$

[14.1.3.10] *Dynamic Item*

10. Identify the parent function for $g(x) = \dfrac{4}{x-4}$.

[A] $y = x$ [B] $y = \dfrac{1}{x}$ [C] $y = \sqrt{x}$ [D] $y = |x|$

Lesson 1: Graphing Functions and Relations

[14.1.3.11] *Dynamic Item*

11. Name the parent function for the graph shown.

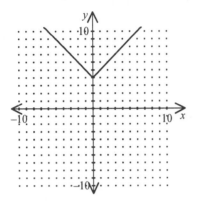

[14.1.3.12] *Dynamic Item*

12. Identify the parent function that can be used to graph the function $f(x) = \dfrac{6}{x-8} + 2$. Do not graph the function.

Lesson 2: Translations

Objective 1: Describe how changes to the rule of a function correspond to the translation of its graph.

[14.2.1.13] *Dynamic Item*

13. Describe how to obtain the graph of $g(x) = (x-4)^2 + 3$ from the parent function $f(x) = x^2$.

[A] 4 units right and 3 units down   [B] 4 units left and 3 units up

[C] 4 units left and 3 units down   [D] 4 units right and 3 units up

Lesson 2: Translations

[14.2.1.14] *Dynamic Item*

14. Find the function whose graph can be obtained by performing the translation 2 units right and 3 units up on the parent function $f(x) = x^2$.

[A] $f(x) = (x-2)^2 + 3$

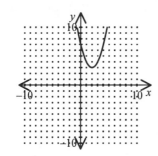

[B] $f(x) = (x-2)^2 - 3$

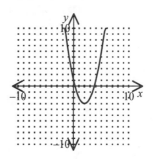

[C] $f(x) = (x+2)^2 + 3$

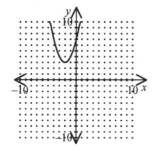

[D] $f(x) = (x+2)^2 - 3$

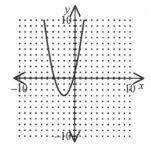

[14.2.1.15] *Dynamic Item*

15. The point $(3, -11)$ is on the graph of a function. What are the coordinates of the corresponding point on the new graph following a horizontal translation of 10.

[14.2.1.16] *Dynamic Item*

16. The point $(2, 4)$ is on the graph of $f(x) = x^2$. Use this fact to describe how $f(x)$ is translated to obtain $g(x) = x^2 - 2$ which contains the point $(2, 2)$.

Lesson 3: Stretches and Compressions

Objective 1: Describe how changes to the rule of a function stretch or compress its graph.

[14.3.1.17] *Dynamic Item*

17. Which of the following is a vertical stretch of the parent graph $f(x) = x^2$?

[A] $g(x) = \frac{1}{4}x^2$ [B] $g(x) = \left(\frac{1}{4}x\right)^2$ [C] $g(x) = (4x)^2$ [D] $g(x) = 4x^2$

[14.3.1.18] *Dynamic Item*

18. Which of the following is a horizontal stretch of the parent graph $f(x) = x^2$?

[A] $g(x) = (2x)^2$ [B] $g(x) = \left(\frac{1}{2}x\right)^2$ [C] $g(x) = 2x^2$ [D] $g(x) = \frac{1}{2}x^2$

[14.3.1.19] *Dynamic Item*

19. Graph on the same plane $f(x) = x^2$ and $g(x) = \frac{1}{4}x^2$.

[14.3.1.20] *Dynamic Item*

20. Graph on the same plane $f(x) = \sqrt{x}$ and $g(x) = \sqrt{4x}$.

Lesson 4: Reflections

Objective 1: Describe how a change to the rule of a function corresponds to a reflection of its graph.

[14.4.1.21] *Dynamic Item*

21. Which of these functions is the reflection of $f(x) = |x|$ across the x-axis?

[A] $g(x) = |-x+1|$ [B] $g(x) = -|x+1|$ [C] $g(x) = -|x|$ [D] $g(x) = |-x|$

Lesson 4: Reflections

[14.4.1.22] *Dynamic Item*

22. Which of these functions is the reflection of $f(x) = x^2$ across the y-axis?

   [A] $g(x) = -x^2$ [B] $g(x) = -(x)^{-2}$ [C] $g(x) = x^{-2}$ [D] $g(x) = (-x)^2$

[14.4.1.23] *Dynamic Item*

23. Graph the pair of functions and identify the transformation. $f(x) = |x| + 4$, $g(x) = |-x| + 4$

[14.4.1.24] *Dynamic Item*

24. Below is the graph of a function $f(x)$. Graph $f(-x)$.

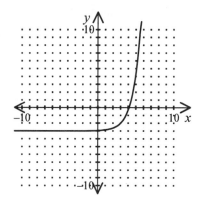

Lesson 5: Combining Transformations

Objective 1: Study a real-world application of transformed functions.

[14.5.1.25] *Dynamic Item*

25. The amount of profit a retail store made each year from 1970 to 2000 is given by the function $p(t) = 4t^2 + 25,000$, where $t = 0$ represents 1970. Which is the model for this function if $t = 0$ represents 1995?

[A] $p(t) = 4(t+25)^2 - 25,000$ [B] $p(t) = 4(t-25)^2 + 25,000$

[C] $p(t) = 4(t-25)^2 - 25,000$ [D] $p(t) = 4(t+25)^2 + 25,000$

[14.5.1.26] *Dynamic Item*

26. The graph for a hotel which charges a $100 flat fee plus $15 per person for a banquet is shown below. How will the graph change if the hotel then changes its policy to a flat fee of $350 plus $20 per person?

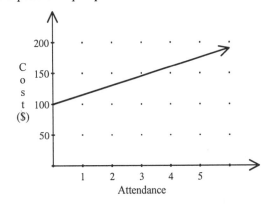

[A] The slope will be 15 and the y-intercept will be 350.

[B] The slope will be 350 and the y-intercept will be 100.

[C] The slope will be 20 and the y-intercept will be 350.

[D] The slope will be 350 and the y-intercept will be 20.

Lesson 5: Combining Transformations

[14.5.1.27] *Dynamic Item*

27. A stable charges a $6 flat fee plus $30 per hour for trail rides.
    a. Write the function that describes the cost, *c*, that a person must pay in order to ride a certain number of hours, *h*.
    b. Identify the parent function.
    c. Describe how the graph of the function from part a is different from the graph of the parent function.

[14.5.1.28] *Dynamic Item*

28. You are planning a 100 mile bike ride, allowing 2 hours for rest stops.
    a. Identify the parent function.
    b. Write the function that describes the rate, *r*, that must be traveled in order to arrive in a certain number of hours, *h*.
    c. Graph both functions.

Objective 2: Graph functions that involve more than one transformation.

[14.5.2.29] *Dynamic Item*

29. Which of the following transformations have been applied to the graph of the parent function, $y = x^2$, to produce the graph of the function $y = 0.5(x+5)^2 - 2$?

    [A] horizontal translation of +5, vertical translation of 2, vertical compression by a factor of 0.5

    [B] reflection across the x-axis, horizontal translation of −5, vertical translation of −2, vertical stretch by a factor of 5

    [C] reflection across the x-axis, horizontal translation of −5, vertical translation of 2, vertical stretch by a factor of 5

    [D] horizontal translation of −5, vertical translation of −2, vertical compression by a factor of 0.5

Lesson 5: Combining Transformations

[14.5.2.30] *Dynamic Item*

30. Given the graph of $f(x) = |x|$, which is the graph of $y = \dfrac{1}{4}|x+2| - 2$?

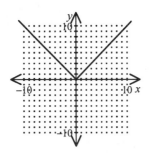

[A]

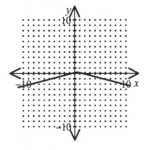

[B]

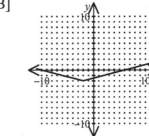

[C]

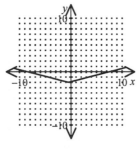

[D]

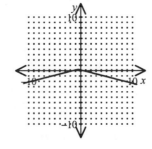

[14.5.2.31] *Dynamic Item*

31. Sketch a graph of the function $f(x) = -\dfrac{1}{x+2}$.

Lesson 5: Combining Transformations

[14.5.2.32] *Dynamic Item*

32. The following transformations are applied to point $A\left(-6, -\dfrac{2}{3}\right)$ in the given order. What are the coordinates of the point that is the final result of these transformations?

    a reflection across the x-axis
    a horizontal translation of 2
    a vertical stretch of 3
    a vertical translation of –4
    a reflection across the y-axis

Lesson 1: Graphing Functions and Relations

Objective 1: Use models to understand functions and relations.

[14.1.1.1] *Dynamic Item*

[1] [C]

[14.1.1.2] *Dynamic Item*

[2] [B]

[14.1.1.3] *Dynamic Item*

[3] $\{(-6,-3),(-5,-3),(-1,-3),(4,-3)\}$; It is a function.

[14.1.1.4] *Dynamic Item*

[4] d: $\{5,\ 6,\ 7,\ 8\}$; r: $\{25,\ 36,\ 49,\ 64\}$

Objective 2: Evaluate functions by using function rules.

[14.1.2.5] *Dynamic Item*

[5] [D]

[14.1.2.6] *Dynamic Item*

[6] [A]

[14.1.2.7] *Dynamic Item*

Domain: all real numbers
[7] Range: all nonpositive real numbers

[14.1.2.8] *Dynamic Item*

[8] 27

Objective 3: Identify the parent functions of some important families of functions.

[14.1.3.9] *Dynamic Item*

[9] [C]

[14.1.3.10] *Dynamic Item*

[10] [B]

[14.1.3.11] *Dynamic Item*

[11] $y = |x|$

[14.1.3.12] *Dynamic Item*

[12] $f(x) = \dfrac{1}{x}$

Lesson 2: Translations

Objective 1: Describe how changes to the rule of a function correspond to the translation of its graph.

[14.2.1.13] *Dynamic Item*

[13] [D]

[14.2.1.14] *Dynamic Item*

[14] [A]

[14.2.1.15] *Dynamic Item*

[15] $(13, -11)$

[14.2.1.16] *Dynamic Item*

[16] The graph is moved down 2 units so the point $(2, 4)$ is moved down 2 units.

Lesson 3: Stretches and Compressions

Objective 1: Describe how changes to the rule of a function stretch or compress its graph.

[14.3.1.17] *Dynamic Item*

[17] [D]

[14.3.1.18] *Dynamic Item*

[18] [B]

[14.3.1.19] *Dynamic Item*

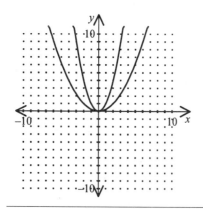

[19]

[14.3.1.20] *Dynamic Item*

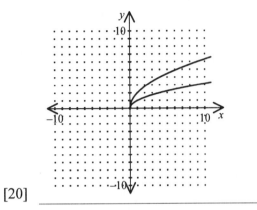

[20] _____

Lesson 4: Reflections

Objective 1: Describe how a change to the rule of a function corresponds to a reflection of its graph.

[14.4.1.21] *Dynamic Item*

[21] [C]

[14.4.1.22] *Dynamic Item*

[22] [D]

[14.4.1.23] *Dynamic Item*

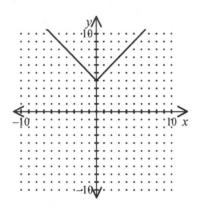

[23]   reflection across the *y*-axis

[14.4.1.24] *Dynamic Item*

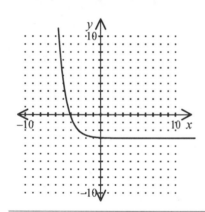

[24]

Lesson 5: Combining Transformations

Objective 1: Study a real-world application of transformed functions.

[14.5.1.25] *Dynamic Item*

[25] [D]

[14.5.1.26] *Dynamic Item*

[26] [C]

[14.5.1.27] *Dynamic Item*

a. $c = 30h + 6$

b. $c = h$

[27] c. The graph is translated 6 units up and stretched vertically by a factor of 30.

[14.5.1.28] *Dynamic Item*

a) $r = \dfrac{1}{h}$

b) $r = \dfrac{100}{h-2}$

c)

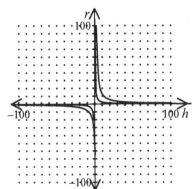

[28] (The parent graph is the one closest to the origin.)

Objective 2: Graph functions that involve more than one transformation.

[14.5.2.29] *Dynamic Item*

[29] [D]

[14.5.2.30] *Dynamic Item*

[30] [B]

[14.5.2.31] *Dynamic Item*

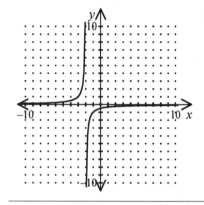

[31]

[14.5.2.32] *Dynamic Item*

[32] (4, –2).